START YOUR OWN

eLEARNING OR TRAINING BUSINESS

Additional titles in **Entrepreneur's Startup Series**

Start Your Own

Entrepreneur
MAGAZINE'S

STARTUP

START YOUR OWN

eLEARNING
OR TRAINING
BUSINESS

YOUR STEP-BY-STEP
GUIDE TO SUCCESS

The Staff of Entrepreneur Media, Inc. & Cheryl Kimball

with Ciree Linsenman

Ep
Entrepreneur
PRESS®

Entrepreneur Press, Publisher
Cover Design: Andrew Welyczko
Production and Composition: Eliot House Productions

Library of Congress Cataloging-in-Publication Data
Kimball, Cheryl, author.
    Start your own eLearning or training business : your step-by-step guide to success / The Staff of Entrepreneur Media and Cheryl Kimball with Ciree Linsenman.
        pages cm.—(Startup series)
        ISBN-13: 978-1-59918-573-6 (paperback)
        ISBN-10: 1-59918-573-3
        1. Continuing education—Marketing. 2. Education and training services industry.
    3. Computer-assisted instruction. I. Linsenman, Ciree, author. II. Entrepreneur Press, author.
    III. Title.
    LC5225.M37.K56 2015
    374—dc23   2015022203

Printed in the United States of America

20 19 18 17 16 15   10 9 8 7 6 5 4 3 2 1

Contents

Chapter 4
Make It Official 53

Chapter 5
A Wealth of Resources 69

Chapter 9
Human Resources 123

Chapter 10
Give Great Content 143

Preface

Europe and the United States have embraced "correspondence education" since the mid-19th century. Women in particular were encouraged to study at home. An online article (untitled) on the history of distance learning by the Interactive Media Lab/University of Florida, says that by the early 20th century along with the delivery of educational materials through the postal service came "instructional radio." While getting an education via radio never quite caught on, digital applications at the other end of that century—what we know as "eLearning"—has become the next dimension of distance learning. Not only is it a success by any measure, the industry is still in its infancy making it a perfect entrepreneurial opportunity.

In *Start Your Own eLearning and Training Business*, we show you how to become part of that success story and that upward trajectory. And the story has many chapters—being involved with eLearning can range from teaching your own classes via the internet, putting together an online learning program, or being in the behind-the-scenes part of the industry working with the platforms that make remote education possible. You can train military personnel, children, the corporate workforce, or the individual looking for personal enrichment. As usual in entrepreneurship, the world is your oyster!

The junction where great technological advancements meet innovative educators and groundbreaking insights into learning psychology is where distance learning is today. And that means while wide open and potentially lucrative, like any startup business, starting your own eLearning business is not for the faint of heart. The distance learning professionals interviewed for this book stressed the importance of defining your top-quality product and competitive edge against thinly built products that are looking to jump onto the crowded online education bus. With easy access to setting up a business structure and a do-it-yourself website, the internet is teeming with people who want to be in the distance learning business.

But despite being crowded, this is a fast-paced marketplace; for those who have exciting ideas, there is a rich field of opportunity with talented people who can help you, fund you, inspire you, and mentor you. And students of life are awaiting the next development in this industry, rapidly consuming all of what is offered to them. It's clear that eLearning methods are holding their own and even dominating some areas of traditional education, such as in retention levels with self-paced learning.

As with an entrepreneurial startup that has a strong work-from-home or at least work independently slant, the eLearning world has become increasingly sophisticated in reaching out to a widespread community and providing opportunities for comradery and collegial interaction with others in the industry. For example, the United States Distance Learning Association offers a conference and comprehensive website where support and information through membership can enhance any online educator's experience. They claim to focus on being working professionals not educational theorists—real-world solutions opposed to educational jargon. This is a community where, they say, the college professor is open to the potential of learning something from the elementary school teacher.

Widespread internet use has proven that we can get and give information as quickly as we think of it. Rapid ascent of the use of mobile devices has replaced much of the stationary exchange of global information to add a whole new element to instant learning—"roving education" is now a trend! Although it may seem almost impossible to keep up with the latest in this ever-changing industry, what you, the potential eLearning entrepreneur, need to focus on is thoughtful, quality development of distance education and how to offer it to the right audiences via the best medium at the moment.

A maturing industry offers some perspective and opportunity to analyze where we have been and where we should go. Innovators are changing the way we think about eLearning by bringing decades-long ideas to fruition with timing that strikes while technology is hot, and delivering them to an audience that is ready to devour the best that comes along. Use the industry tools mentioned throughout this book to keep abreast of the next new thing and jump on board when the time is right for your product and the learners you have chosen to target. Don't let the rapid-changing technology scare you—adapt or not, and as quickly or slowly as your market seems to respond. After all, despite the saturation of electronic devices through almost all demographics, pencils and paper are still made and sold! A solid foundational tool will outlast fads and trends.

You'll be able to test what other educators are creating and form opinions about their products as you use them to get seasoned, certified, and ready for business. If you wish to get your feet wet working for an existing educational product, a resounding "no" was the answer when we asked distance educators whether standard degrees and qualifications determine whom they hire and work with. Professionals in this field seem to be a rich collage of life experiences rather than just standard degrees on a resume, which means that if you have the right skills and a self-propelled drive for knowledge, you can thrive.

This is a perfect industry in which you can start slow and build. No need to jump out of the box with massive startup debt. Using the wisdom in the upcoming pages, you can create and focus on your own custom plan. Step-by-measured-step using educated, calculated moves, you can move beyond the intimidation phase and surface as a key player in this exciting, evolving arena!

Online Learning Today

Students of life are thriving on the technological advancements that allow them to absorb information efficiently with a whole host of advantages over primarily attending physical, actual classrooms. Distance learning focuses on brain-to-brain transmission of information, allowing learners to save time and money. But where is the place for in-person learning after we embrace the light speed at which information is gleaned for better, more, and most current information? The fusion of face-to-face and distance learning is a fine art and there is a place for both. Each compliments the other and brings to the table qualities the other cannot for an end result that is better than each alone. Adapting the latest technology to the most recent understandings of the way people learn and creating courses that are an appropriate, balanced mix of simulation and tangible experience is what makes distance training today so exciting and limitless.

Distance Learning Needs

Who can benefit from online learning? The answer is any person with an internet connection and computer, wanting to enrich his or her life with a skill or bit of knowledge. Calculus, the newest club scene dance moves, making gluten-free bread, preparing for SATs, corporate sexual harassment procedures, earning an MBA, food safety, writing a screenplay, mortuary science, witchcraft, smart investing, and programming languages are just the beginning of an endless list.

You, as an eLearning professional, can also benefit enormously from the growing interest in self-improvement and the public's desire to attain higher education degrees and training certifications. Not only will you learn from the research you'll need to do to constantly improve your coursework, you'll also learn from the wide array of context in which you'll teach and, of course, from what each student brings to the table.

▶ EdTech Distilled

Educational technology, otherwise known as "EdTech," is the rapidly developing field dedicated to improving and promoting education through the development of tools such as software, hardware, and teaching processes. It is the mate of distance learning. It combines the skills of high-art technical minds and educators who excel in disseminating knowledge to bring ever more improved ways for students to receive education. It layers face-to-face assistance from great minds in education with online mentorship and learning games programmed to adapt and customize as learners navigate through its systems.

EdTech is advancing and developing trends and tools in each of the main four markets of distance learning: children and young adult education, higher education, corporate training and professional development, and personal enrichment courses.

More than ever, learning at the pace of the student—whether that student is striving for an advanced degree, corporate or technical skill, or personal enrichment—is very appealing as the pace of absorbing information quickens and our conditioning to convenience grows. Combining training methods and matching each to the venue that is most practical and sensible for it makes for higher quality learning than can be achieved only in person; saving time by watching a technical demonstration video from home rather than driving to see an instructor give the demo serves to budget room for those things that are best experienced in person, such as interactive lectures and forums that involve subtly nuanced contributions of everyone in the room. Being able to view certain parts of a self-paced (asynchronous) lesson over and over customizes the lesson to the student and can reduce stress and increase absorption, allowing learners to achieve higher scores on tests.

stat fact

eLearning Industry, the largest online community of professionals involved in the eLearning industry (elearningindustry.com), estimates the online education market to reach $107 billion by the end of 2015 and self-paced distance learning revenues to comprise $49.9 billion of that figure.

Feed the Need

People are being conditioned by the fast pace of digital communication and quick absorption of facts when they want them, and there is pressure to be aware of more and more information as it becomes available. Mobile devices are being used both purposefully and on the fly to complete whole or segments of courses as they continue to be the dominant online platform. "MLearning," or mobile learning, is also forecasted to be the dominant way people choose to engage in distance learning. Employers expect further education to save them time and money with employees' improved efficiency. Children and young adults are naturals at learning new technologies and schools that implement distance learning capabilities afford them a chance to excel further than with traditional classrooms alone, with the ability to access information across the world with the click of the mouse. Income-challenged

stat fact

International Society for Technology in Education's 2014 survey reveals that three-quarters of K–12 respondents say technology integration is highly important, but their current levels and ideal levels of integration do not align: Only 22 percent say their schools are already highly integrated.

▶ The Future of eLearning Design

It's in the fate of the numbers. Learning can be had on a train, on a plane, at a bus stop, or in a hospital bed with those precious waiting moments we all have. Gartner, Inc., a technology research company, says mobile phones are expected to dominate overall device shipments and forecasts 2015 purchasing numbers of computer and other mobile devices as follows:

- ▶ PC (desk and notebook): 268,491
- ▶ Ultra mobile tablets: 324,565
- ▶ Mobile phones: 1,964,788
- ▶ Hybrid and clamshell mobiles: 63,835

Forecasted 2015 numbers of shipments by operating system tell another story important to eLearning design:

- ▶ Android: 1,254,367
- ▶ Windows: 422,726
- ▶ iOS/Mac OS: 397,234
- ▶ RIM: 10,597
- ▶ Chrome: 8,000
- ▶ Others: 528,755

Gartner's research director Ranjit Atwal says, "The device market continues to evolve, with buyers deciding which combination of devices is required to meet their wants and needs. Mobile phones are a must have and will continue to grow but at a slower pace, with opportunities moving away from the top-end premium devices to mid-end basic products. Meanwhile, users continue to move away from the traditional PC (notebooks and desk-based) as it becomes more of a shared content creation tool, while the greater flexibility of tablets, hybrids, and lighter notebooks address users' increasingly different demands."

and rural students sometimes attend schools with limited offerings and distance learning can bring a gifted student advanced courses her school may not offer, or supplemental courses to homeschoolers.

Adults and children with leisure time and a budget to enjoy it are opting for personal enrichment through distance learning in many areas. Making art and art appreciation, social skills, psychology topics, relationship counseling, yoga, and learning foreign languages are just some of the areas learners are seeking fun and stimulation online. Adults often go back

▶ Higher Education Right Now

EdX.org is a nonprofit, higher education portal focusing on the way students learn. Time is the only limit you'll have with learning on the edX site. This organization offers both free courses and audited course versions of MOOCs (massive open online courses) with an Honor Code Certificate or Verified Certificates of Achievement for a small fee for many of these online classes from major universities. Here is a sampling:

- ▶ Positive Behavior Support for Young Children, University of Washington
- ▶ The Civil War and Reconstruction, Columbia University
- ▶ The Ethics of Eating, Cornell University
- ▶ The Engineering of Structures Around Us, Dartmouth College
- ▶ The Fascinating World of Robots and Robotics, University of Peking
- ▶ The Science of Happiness, University of California, Berkeley
- ▶ Understanding Wireless Technology, Economics, and Policy, University of Notre Dame
- ▶ Visualizing Postwar Tokyo, University of Tokyo

Here are some more places to take MOOCs:

- ▶ www.udacity.com
- ▶ www.coursera.org
- ▶ https://iversity.org
- ▶ www.udemy.com
- ▶ www.open.edu/itunes/

to subjects covered in high school and college with new interest; the abundance of free and low-cost university courses offered online can make taking typically mandatory classes for a degree seem like something interesting and fun, just because.

Corporate Training

Corporate training has a big pocketbook and many needs to fill. According to *Forbes'* 2014 Corporate Learning Factbook, U.S. spending on corporate training rose to over $70 billion in 2013, a 15 percent increase from 2012. Worldwide training spending was $130 billion. These large numbers are a great indicator of positive economic activity and reflect our growing priorities: higher demands for capability, leadership, and deeper knowledge on the job. Forbes reports "capability gaps" exist in 70 percent of the businesses surveyed as well as the very slow development and return on investment when hiring experienced professionals; they really don't perform at 100 percent for the company until they've been there for five years. Skills such as leadership, technical functions and upgrades, customer service, industry- and job-specific fine-tuning are just some of the ways employers are further training their teams.

Children and Young Adults

Kindergarten through 12th grade students are large users of eLearning, and the investment they make in

stat fact

Docebo, a software-as-a-service/learning management system (SaaS/LMS) company, reports large and small corporations, startup entrepreneurs, and universities of all sizes invested $6 billion of venture capital into eLearning over the past five years.

► Global eLearning Earnings

Salaries around the world reflect dollars spent on distance learning. The eLearning Guild's "2014 Global eLearning Salary & Compensation Report" shows average salaries around the world. Look at the chart below to see how the U.S. ranks against other countries.

Australia: $94,665

New Zealand: $69,919

United States: $78,932

North and South America excluding U.S. and Canada: $47,961

Canada: $79,153

Netherlands: $97,295

Europe: $67,738

United Kingdom: $70,871

Asia, excluding India: $52,656

India: $33,743

Africa: $41,951

Other: $63,431

Overall global average: $76,530

adapting to the technology paves the way to lifelong distance learning, later using it for vocational training, continuing adult education, and, of course, college and on-the-job skills. Thinking about your current students as students for life will help you shape what and how you offer your courses and the core skills attached to them.

The results of a 12-year report gleaned from 99 studies conducted by the U.S. Department of Education revealed that students doing some or all of a course online ranked in the 59th percentile compared with the students who took the same course solely in traditional classrooms and ranked in the 50th percentile. Barbara Means, the study's lead author, says it demonstrates how much better online learning can serve students and that it is better than conventional instruction. Read the full report here: www.ed.gov/rschstat/ eval/tech/evidence-based-practices/finalreport.pdf.

Thirty states now provide full online learning to all in-state resident students, with attendance at a 6.2 percent increase over 2013, meeting the needs of 315,000 students enrolling in 740,000 courses to which they otherwise may not have access (www.kpk12. com/wp-content/uploads/EEG_KP2014-fnl-lr.pdf). States are authorizing "innovation zones" that give schools new advantages and the flexibility to develop, learn, and use online teaching methods in their curricula. Learning centers offer one-to-one teacher-student conferencing and high tech synchronous (real time) support to students. Digital learning in charter schools provides custom training and support to teachers who otherwise lack experience, and at-home tutoring to high school students at risk of dropping out.

▶ Distance Education Defined

The terms "distance education" and "distance learning" are often used liberally with varying definitions. The Association for Talent Development (ATD, formerly ASTD), a premiere network resource for training and educational development professionals, defines distance education as an "educational situation in which the instructor and students are separated by time, location, or both. Education or training courses are delivered to remote locations via synchronous or asynchronous means of instruction, including written correspondence, text, graphics, audio and video, CD-ROM, online learning, audio- and videoconferencing, interactive TV, and fax. Distance education does not preclude the use of the traditional classroom. The definition of distance education is broader and entails the definition of eLearning."

Personal Enrichment

The retirement age of 65 is fading into the sunset as the new 65 becomes healthier and more active, as well as needing to pay bills for a longer duration. Eight out of ten baby boomers say they plan to work at least part time after they reach that age. They are training for second and third careers, enhancing their lives with personal fulfillment classes online, and participating in brain training challenges such as those at Lumosity (www.lumosity. com) to keep their brains pliable and ready for action. Because seniors are often mobility challenged, obtaining these many knowledge gifts through face-to-face learning would present a challenge. Incorporating the speed of online delivery systems helps save precious time, boosts social skills, and offers a wide knowledge base that keeps homebound brains stimulated and healthier.

The Roots of Distance Learning

The roots of education from afar can be traced back to many places, as forms of information were exchanged via snail mail, telephone, radio, and TV. Searching for "the history of distance learning" will unearth different accounts of the many steps that led to where we are today. Here are just a few of the contributors:

▶ 1858—The University of London was the first to offer an external study program in which students could and may still earn undergraduate and postgraduate degrees, at low cost, on completion of testing at global centers. Providing educational status for the income-challenged and study-by-mail for British POWS were two large contributions made by University of London. Many prisoners earned degrees while in captivity.

▶ 1891—William Rainey Harper, the first president of the University of Chicago, pushed the movement along by encouraging continuing education by correspondence. A training program originally intended for coal miners eventually became the International Correspondence Schools. These distance schools multiplied rapidly due to aggressive selling and the appeal of receiving whole textbooks instead of single lessons.

▶ 1920s—Education radio begins, showing how many can learn from a great distance.

▶ 1940s—Television broadcasts educational information to the public. Sir Isaac Pitman, the inventor of shorthand, taught his students by mail. He mailed his students assignments in the form of postcards, read and corrected their mailed assignments, then sent them tutelage.

► 1954 to 1970—National Educational Television (NET), owned by the Ford Foundation and the Corporation for Public Broadcasting, provided viewers with five hours per day of in-depth education richly guided by historical and literary pillars, a stark contrast to what was being offered on all the other channels that had commercials and programming based purely on entertainment value. NET offered raw documentaries, gritty coverage of social issues such as racism and poverty, and gained a reputation for being a liberal "University of the Air. After controversy about the documentary subjects, in 1970 PBS reformed many of NET's offerings and took over providing viewers educational TV.

► 1971—Britain offers the opportunity to anyone with access to the internet to earn a master's degree through the Open University.

► 1985—James Milojkovic, Ph.D., and TeleLearning, Inc. create The Electronic University Network. "[This was] in essence the world's first online university where adult students could take a core set of college-level courses and gain college credit [by] passing CLEP exams. This was well before the ubiquity of the internet, the world wide web, and high-speed broadband connections. Our students worked on the first personal computers such as the Apple IIe, Commodore 64, and, of course, the IBM PC. They accessed the network via a dial-up connection with 300-baud modems and were thrilled when 1200-baud modems became available! Our vision was 30 years ahead of its time," says Milo (Milojkovic). See Figure 1–1 on page 10.

► 1991 to 1994—The oldest online K–12 school in the U.S., Laurel Springs, starts in 1991 and develops its online curriculum in 1994.

► 1995—Two webcast developments hit the scene: Benford E. Standley produced one of the first audio/video webcasts in history, and Apple Computer's Webcasting Group helped launch the Macintosh New York Music Festival.

► 1997—The term "eLearning" surfaces, possibly at a computer-based training seminar, referring to distance learning, and later to include online, virtual, personalized, interactive education.

► 2000—The Florida Virtual School offers free education to 600,000 K–12 students.

► 2006—Stanford University Online High School serves supplemental courses for gifted students grades 7 through 12.

► 2011—Global Online Academy offers 53 schools in 24 states online courses.

stat fact

According to Skilledup.com, worldwide eLearning revenues are expected to grow to $51.5 billion by 2016, an annual growth rate of 7.6 percent.

NETWORK NEWS

STUDENT NEWS FROM THE ELECTRONIC UNIVERSITY NETWORK
• A DIVISION OF TELELEARNING, INC. •

Volume 1, Issue 1   Fall 1986

Network Introduces "Protégé"

Dr. James Milojkovic, Tele-Learning's Vice President of Research and Development, announced the availability of a new computer-telecommunicated instruction system called "Protégé," which he believes goes further to revolutionize higher education programs than any other single system available. During a taping of a PBS television program dealing with technological advances affecting the home computer industry ("The Computer Chronicles," syndicated nationally on over 160 PBS stations), Milojkovic unveiled plans to launch a pilot program involving a limited number of Electronic University Network courses this fall. A major implementation of the Protégé system is scheduled for January, 1987.

Three Years in Development

"For three years, our research teams, technology experts, program designers and educators have wrestled with the development of a system that would fulfill the promised educational breakthrough futurists have predicted would be available before the end of this century," Milojkovic said. For years, commentators like Alvin Toffler and John Naisbitt have hinted that technology would eventually be able to solve the escalating "crisis in education" which has been the focus of governmental and media attention since the launching of Sputnik.

We live in an information society yet the traditional educational system does not reflect that fact. With ever increasing technological change and growth, the average person may have to retrain to remain productive several times throughout the course of a career. Our educational system has to help learners shift from product to process: from "what is to be learned" to "how to learn and think."

Conventional computer-assisted instruction (CAI) has not been an effective solution. By its very nature, CAI isolates the student from human teachers and has often been little more than dry electronic page turning or drill-and-practice routines. Enormous expenditures of time and money are required for the production of high quality programs which are still more the exception than the rule.

Greater Flexibility

Protégé was developed for the specific purpose of providing an expert instructor with the flexibility to design and deliver a maximally effective educational experience. The Protégé software allows for flexible and ongoing communication between instructor and student on lessons and assignments.   Protégé uses the personal computer BOTH as a communications device and as a

Dr. James Milojkovic introduces 'Protégé.'

presentation medium for a knowledge acquisition system that enables students to learn and assimilate new knowledge as they demonstrate depth of understanding. Because of its modular conception, Protégé courses can include and take advantage of the entire spectrum of educational media.

Based on "Master Teacher" Concept

The Protégé system captures recognized master teaching techniques in a computer format with graphic template structures. These "knowledge templates" engage students in learning activities that center on organizing thoughts, formulating opinions, challenging other's ideas, and drawing conclusions.   They encourage active learning that builds the crucial skills involved with both critical and creative thinking.

The scope of the educational experience is limited only by the vision of the instructor. In essence, the instructor serves as a mentor who personally guides the learning

of a protégé.   Since the underlying technology of the Protégé system is telecommunication, this personalized guidance can occur regardless of location or life/work schedules. The system allows the student to communicate with his or her instructor at any time during a course.

"Our guiding philosophy in the technical design of the Protégé system was to make the technology as transparent as possible for the adult learner," Milojkovic pointed out.   The software is menu driven with informational prompts and error messages all in plain English. Context sensitive help screens are available throughout the system.   All telecommunication protocols and complex sign-ons are automated and available through the simple press of one key.   "We wanted the student to concentrate on mastering the coursework rather than agonizing with the educationally irrelevant complexities of computers and telecommunication. The results of our beta-testing confirm that we have produced a truly 'learner-friendly' system."

FIGURE 1–1: **The Online University Network**
This historic document is a newsletter from 1986 announcing the new telecommunications software system Milojkovic designed for the Protégé (the student software system) to work with Mentor (the professor's software system).

▶ 2013 to 2014—Online School for Girls, a consortium of 83 schools, offers 7 summer and 20 school-year courses.

Today, keeping on budget and transferring information quickly across the miles play a large role in how eLearning is used. When you call your local utility company to pay a bill or order service and wind up speaking with someone in another country, chances are that person is an outsourced employee, well trained by a distance learning program. Corporate outsourced services training comprises 42 percent of corporate training expenditures. Corporations are now more apt to reinvest in current employees who lag behind in skills, bringing them up to speed with online learning rather than investing in a complete fire-hire HR cycle.

Employees are also proactively upping their ante by requesting additional training in-house or using tuition reimbursement programs to build their own programs from varied online sources. Recognizing the role online learning plays in relation to income inspires employees to continually evolve, and when employers see increased results or productivity as a result of continuing education, they too put additional value on further employee training. Opportunities in many industries related to enhancing employee skills are very lucrative.

Ask the Employer: How Much Does It Matter?

In the 2012 "Lifelong Education and Labor Market Needs" study conducted by EvoLLLution, employers expressed how they value ongoing education. When asked if ongoing (after hire) education affects compensation and salary, 87 percent responded "yes" and only 13 percent said "no." Seventy-eight percent felt that ongoing education for employees influences their advancements and promotions within the company, and a resounding 96 percent agreed that it has a positive effect on employee job performance. This, compounded with the fact that 64 percent of externally recruited executives fail within four years of joining the organization, point to all thumbs up for continued training. With stats like these, everyone should be doing it.

Riches in Enrichment

The Encore Career Institute (ECI, www.encore.org) partnered with UCLA Extension School offers a comprehensive online educational career service for seniors,

stat fact

According to a 2014–2016 report produced by Docebo, the highest growth rate for the eLearning market is in Asia at 17.3 percent. Eastern Europe, Africa, and Latin America clock in at 16.9 percent, 15.2 percent, and 14.6 percent, respectively.

▶ Top Reasons Students Choose Online Learning

According to Franklin University, a popular online school, the top six reasons students choose online over traditional schooling are:

1. *Balance.* Saving time by studying when they want helps students stay active in fun activities, family time, and work.

2. *Flexible, go-anywhere studying.* Eating donuts on the couch in your Cookie Monster pajamas gets you just as ready for tests as sitting in a rigid, uncomfortable chair under fluorescent lights.

3. *Accelerated courses and degree programs.* Online classes like those offered at Franklin University often take less than 15 weeks and degree programs are usually faster, too.

4. *Lower costs.* Self-paced learning helps adult learners save on tuition.

5. *Access to earn prestigious credentials.* Ivy League schools now offer online education that students may not have been able to afford in the past and employers like seeing those names on resumes.

6. *Self-paced learning is more effective.* Reducing stress for independent learners helps them achieve better grades and be more productive.

including professional certifications and career counseling to ensure they stay engaged in the job market. Cathy Sandeen, dean of UCLA Extension, understands how valuable the senior workforce is, bringing years of rich experience, training, and knowledge to the platform. According to ECI, over 4.5 million Americans age 50 to 70 are working in second or third careers, (encore roles) today. Right now, 21 million are preparing for those encore roles. That 55 percent of the U.S. population puts a high value on helping others with their skills and expertise, viewing it as an important part of midlife and beyond.

With all of this enthusiasm and success around eLearning, we hope you are excited to get on your way to becoming a profitable, enriching contributor to the movement. Read on to find practical tips for setting up your business that can save you time and money, building a powerful network to foster your growth, creating impressive and stimulating products, and keeping a healthy eye on the future.

Staking Your Claim

There are so many avenues you could take in the eLearning industry that it is critical to spend some time reflecting on what your role might be and asking the right questions to ensure your time is well spent. It's important to know the potential outcomes of executing any major life decision. The experience of the professionals who've given their wisdom to this book will help guide your course.

The Path to Destiny

There are many professions within the eLearning industry. It takes a multifaceted educator to create great coursework, and choosing the "right" identity with which to enter the arena can be unclear. It's more important that you take some preliminary training, then jump in and start learning in either an entry level or open-ended job, than enter the market as a perfectly defined professional. On-the-job learning seems to be what has best served the professionals interviewed for this book, providing foundational stepping stones to their maturation in the industry.

Such is the case of Julie Dirksen of Usable Learning (www.usablelearning.com) in Minneapolis, Minnesota. Professionals working in the training industry often see a way to make the jump to creating eLearning packages on their own. Dirksen was an English major, doing a "bit of training and development" for a corporation and found she loved designing experiences for people. She then went back to school to get a Master of Science degree in Instructional Systems Technology from Indiana University.

Today Dirksen is an independent consultant and instructional designer who creates highly interactive

tip

The Training the Trainer resource pack, a free download sponsored and created by the International Council on Archives, offers guidance in planning, organizing, and delivering effective training for both professionals and support staff, whatever their working or learning environment. It addresses various techniques for delivering training and practical administrative tasks that are essential for successful training courses. Download a free Training the Trainer pack at www.ica-sae.org.

eLearning experiences for Fortune 500 companies, innovative technology startups, and major grant-funded research initiatives. Her focus has been on "utilizing the disciplines of educational psychology, neuroscience, change management, and persuasive technology to promote and support the improvement of peoples' lives through sustainable long-term learning and behavioral change."

Dirksen loves learning and the research for each subject she is assigned enriches her own education. As an instructional design consultant you might find that, like Dirksen, one month might hold research for technical tutorials for fixing machines and company policy courses for an airline, and the next involves studying an entire organization's procedures and group psychology to determine a massive restructuring plan. Do you love learning and research? If so, you may want to be an independent consultant and instructional designer.

It Takes a Village

Look at this list of professions that play a part in rolling an eLearning product out the door, and you'll get an idea of some of the major skills required to make it happen:

▶ *Instructional Designer (ID)*. This is the general contractor of the entire project. The ID is usually the person who has the first point of contact with the client, gathering the needed direction and information to then create an operational guide and style guide for cohesion of the project.

▶ *eLearning Developer*. This person makes the ID's vision come to life with content development, storyboarding, and assigning a structure, or body, to the technological work.

▶ *Learning and Development (L&D) Specialist*. This support position is the human learning management system (LMS) that manages the actual software LMS. With long-range vision, the L&D specialist organizes the overall module and supports and orchestrates the other contributed elements falling into place, sometimes with a big emphasis on technology skills.

▶ *eLearning Consultant*. This person is like the team coach. She helps the team best deliver what the client needs from the start of the creation phase to delivery and maintenance of the product, including choices around technology, branding, style, and language.

▶ *Learning Strategist*. Staying on top of current trends and what the competition is doing makes up part of this person's contribution to the team. Taking those facts and affecting what the team creates in all areas of production is the other half.

▶ *Chief Learning Officer*. Also sometimes called a director of training, this person drives the direction of the whole company in the areas of scope of work decisions, future goals, and company structure and policies.

You may start your company out as an expert in one of these roles but as you offer your training skills to different groups and projects, you'll probably expand your role to encompass additional areas of knowledge essential to creating great work. As you become multifaceted, learning from professionals around you and rising to each new occasion, so do you increase your value to future opportunities. Throughout your career as a distance educator, it's important to update and redefine the addition of these skills to your repertoire in a way the public can see. You can do this by highlighting these skills on your professional profiles such as LinkedIn and trade association sites, and officially adding certifications that validate your new learning.

Diane Elkins and Desiree Pinder met on a contract job building software for a large retailer when they discovered that with their combined skills they'd make a great team.

They used the year on that contract to test the waters with one another, build more connections, and pay their bills while they built up their new venture, Artisan E-Learning (www.artisanelearning.com). Because they were building software together they had an extended opportunity to get to know one another and see if they worked well enough together to form a partnership.

Elkins says that the traits required to do well as an eLearning specialist are drive and an acceptance that you are going to be in job search mode 24/7 trying to round up that next client. "If you are a one-person shop, you have to have a lot of skills to create: course writing, designing video, assembling it all, and project management. That's great if you do, but if you don't you need to partner with someone."

Identify Your Offerings

Identifying your offerings and innate tendencies will help you hone in on which audiences might hold the most opportunity for you to target. After you do that, you can profile your audience, shape your training methods and style, and market your product in the appropriate venues. There are many ways to offer your talents through a curriculum and achieve different goals with them.

You may already understand what it is you'll be offering to students out there in cyber space because you're an active professional in the field of your subject matter, and teaching or talking about what you know may seem natural. Or, you might know that you like teaching and training but are not sure of the subject that best fits your knowledge breadth. Perhaps you like research and are great at assimilating large quantities of information for presentation. Try filling out Figure 2–1 to shine some light on the subject.

Distance learning has many portals and markets that could use your skills. Before outlining your offerings, first get a solid understanding of the primary markets: corporate training, higher education, continuing enrichment and professional education, and child and young adult education. Think about your personality, lifestyle, and working habits and ponder how you might match up with each of these areas.

Corporate Training

Do you enjoy switching your area of study every few months? The array includes training employees for skills in leadership, conflict resolution, corporate strategy, and critical thinking to name just a few. Technical, industry-specific skills training, and new hire orientations for large corporations are more popular needs. Corporate training requires critical listening and implementation skills, teamwork, and the ability to process lots of new

Targeting Your Market Worksheet

► What areas of study have you formally completed? _____

_____

► What are you naturally good at that you may not have studied in school? _____

_____

► Is there a special talent or service that your friends request of you or compliment you on?

_____

► Think back to when you were a child. Do you remember a passion or skill that was lost along the way, as you grew older? _____

_____

► If you had a month of free time and no budget constraints, how would you spend that time and where would you go? Why? _____

_____

► How long can you sit and concentrate on writing, reading, or talking at one time? _____

_____

► What tasks in life do you dread and put off? _____

_____

► List some past projects that have been successful, or that you've felt particularly proud of accomplishing. They can even be decades in your past. What was it about completing that project that felt different than other accomplishments? _____

_____

_____

► Do you currently operate a business or offer a service that might benefit from adding online training as a side service or income stream? How would your training enhance your business? _____

_____

_____

FIGURE 2–1: **Targeting Your Market Worksheet**

Targeting Your Market Worksheet, continued

► Are you currently employed and do you plan to/can you keep your current job full or part time while you test the waters starting your new business? _____

_____

► Are your finances for the next two years clearly allocated or will you need to seek funding to start your business? _____

_____

► Are you tech savvy or do you usually need help figuring out how to use software, hardware, and new web services? _____

_____

► How do you typically chart your day? Will you be able to configure the time slots necessary to run this business into your natural patterns? _____

_____

_____

FIGURE 2–1: **Targeting Your Market Worksheet,** continued

information continually and rapidly, as you work with companies to create ways they can achieve their goals. To lead group training successfully, you need a broad understanding of human behavior. You also need to accept and tolerate many different personalities. Figure 2–2 on page 19 gives you an idea of the state of the industry.

Unflappable You

Sometimes working for busy executives means your scheduled training or meeting dates will be cancelled and rescheduled. In large corporations, securing a direct communication line to all the right people needed to approve a project can be challenging, so wait times to complete your mission may be long. Are you patient, resourceful, forgiving of erratic human behavior, and creatively aggressive about getting what you want?

Directing group discussions online or off requires leadership skills and focus. Sometimes frustrated employees will try to dominate the experience for others by taking

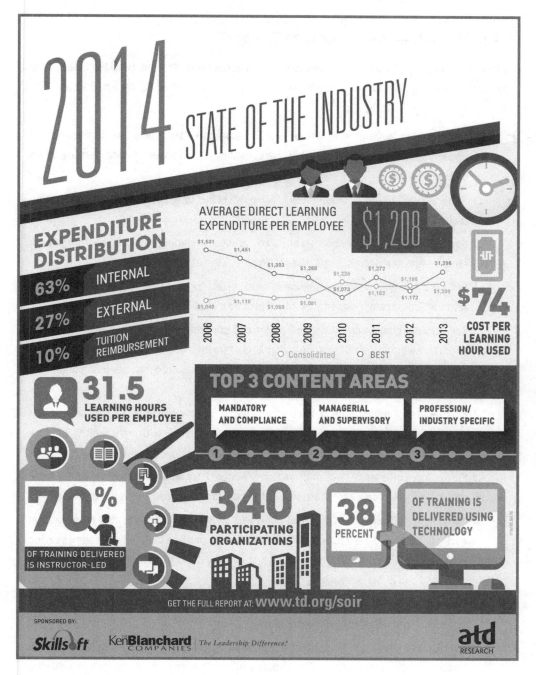

FIGURE 2–2: **2014 State of the Industry**

▶ Are You a Natural Corporate Trainer?

Pearson Higher Education (http://home.pearsonhighered.com) uses this checklist test to help you understand if you and corporate training go together like peanut butter and jelly or water and oil:

- ❑ *Are you able to frequently switch gears?* Be prepared to review course material for upcoming assignments for possibly five seminars in a two-week period that are all on different topics.

- ❑ *Run training seminars.* These often involve travel and long days using vibrant teaching techniques.

- ❑ *Participate in the preparation of course materials.* Developing new courses from scratch requires lots of research, focus, and testing.

- ❑ *Set up of computer labs.* Equipment must often be reconfigured in between labs. Although some companies employ lab aides to do lab set-ups for the instructors, not all do.

- ❑ *Solid time management skills.* You might add speaking engagements and lectures to your course outline, so think about what kind of traveler you are. Cab rides, flights, hotel stays, and getting to your destination on time and unflustered requires being organized and prepared for the unexpected.

- ❑ *Fast learner.* Keeping a quick pace while absorbing new material is important. If you aren't good at this, try some new study techniques, stick with very limited product development, or reconsider this field.

- ❑ *Flexibility.* Equipment that malfunctions, bungled travel arrangements, and people doing what you didn't expect are some of the reasons you need an even temper.

- ❑ *Mastery of skill-based teaching.* Not only do you need to be able to convey new material easily, but you also need to be able to focus learners to a fine point on mastering specific skills and learning technical information fast, so they can continue working. This requires a focused and directive teaching style.

- ❑ *Sense of humor.* Being able to laugh makes you more approachable, diffuses awkward situations, and helps learners feel relaxed.

- ❑ *Enthusiasm.* If you are passionate about what you're doing, your enthusiasm should come through even when you're tired. If you aren't enthusiastic about your subjects, learners won't be either.

the set discussion subjects off course. Do you have the affinity to use intelligent humor and great storytelling skills to reel attention back in? If you are easily irritated by people and think you can mostly stay behind the safety of your computer in your pajamas slurping java, reconsider. Most online corporate training does well to follow the flipped classroom model, incorporating a few live, face-to-face sessions for enthusiastic discussions and presentations.

So, do you still think you might want to be a corporate trainer? Get ready to get certified. You may not need certifications to train professionals but having them increases your chances of getting hired and doing a better job. Check out the certifications section in Chapter 3 to plan your studies.

Higher Education

Distance learning greatly challenges the definition of traditional higher education. With more than seven million students defaulting on their student loans, and the average rise of tuition at universities and colleges at a steady tick of 27 percent per year, more value-priced distance education is getting fair play. Statistics presented by the University of the Potomac compare the average cost of a higher education degree the traditional way at $85,000 to a $30,000 average for an equal education online.

With the popularity of massive open online classes (MOOCs), which are often free, students can take classes from prestigious colleges and universities. A study by edX (www.edX.org), an online learning resource project governed by MIT and Harvard, showed that in 2012 and 2013 138,000 Americans enrolled in MOOCs and topped the global charts with their lust for free higher learning, followed by Europe at 72,000 enrollment and India at 60,000. Slightly more men than women take MOOCs and usage by level of education is evenly spread from secondary education or below, through bachelors and post-graduate degrees. Websites like Open Culture list free courses from top Universities such as Stanford, Berkeley, Yale, Harvard, and MIT. View their list of 1,100 free courses here: www.openculture.com/freeonlinecourses.

Give Them What They Crave

Just studying how markets behave isn't enough to direct your career path. It's important to stay on top of which products within the markets are most sought after, and what related products the same market uses. The higher education crowd consumes massive amounts of test prep services for the GMAT (www.gmac.com/gmat.aspx), GRE (www.kaptest.com/gre), and LSAT (www.petersons.com).

► Doing Business with the Whiz Kids

Training magazine (www.trainingmag.com) creates an annual Training Top 125 list of companies that do impressive things with their training budgets. Studying this list and the companies that invest heavily in training will give you an edge on your market research if you intend to offer corporate training. Look at the list below to see the first ten and study the rest of big corporate training investors here: www.trainingmag.com/sites/default/files/2014_01_Training_Top_125_1.pdf

- ► Jiffy Lube® International, Inc. has 20,500 employees and 6,000 regular trainers spread throughout the U.S. They enabled employees to earn 148,000 technical skill certifications in 2012 and their current training hours have more than doubled since then. Employees in 89 percent of Jiffy Lube stores are certified at an 80-percent level or above.

- ► Keller Williams Realty, Inc. employs over 90,000 in the U.S. and trains its sales staff, with the BOLD program, to be relentless by conditioning them with mindset exercises, language techniques, and lead generation tactics. BOLD uses accountability teams to ensure participants stay on track. Last year those who graduated increased their income by 114 percent and closed 50 percent more transactions.

- ► Capital Blue Cross employs 1,917 in the U.S. and focuses on a proven leadership attributes program to assess participants undergoing the training challenges. One of the training locations (seven sessions in a one-year span) is the dramatic Gettysburg National Battlefield. Positive changes as a result of the program are 100 percent increase in collaboration willingness, promotions to greater leadership responsibility for 75 percent of participants, and 80 percent of participants increased readiness to move up the ladder.

- ► CHG Healthcare Services employs 1,784 in the U.S. Its Lean program trains employees through work sessions. This training has contributed to a 20 percent revenue growth for CHG and in 2015 eliminated 1,626 process steps, saved 20,168 labor hours, and avoided 41 process mistakes, totaling a $7.3 million cost savings. Employees voted their company to the number three position on *Fortune*'s "100 Best Companies to Work For" list.

- ► Mohawk Industries, Inc. employs 19,759 U.S. workers and focuses its training on a "zero landfill" goal by coaching from recycling stream experts. Four of its manufacturing sites eliminated all waste in 2013 and saved millions of dollars in revenue, as well as prevented tons of waste from entering landfills.

All of these companies offer tuition reimbursement programs. Even though the impressive training programs they are using are somewhat industry specific, companies like these support new training ideas and helping employees earn additional certificates for professional growth. Knowing they want employees to be all they can be, what could you offer to these venues?

Students spend thousands on higher education degrees and still find the job market reeks of a stagnating economy. *The Wall Street Journal* poses the idea that if students took the approximately $174,000 required to obtain a Harvard M.B.A. and invested in themselves, via investment in their top educational priorities, à la complete life immersion, there would be a greater reward than the traditional road yields. It suggests to the student that they spend their education budget on moving to the area of the country where things really sizzle in their area of interest, spending quality time hobnobbing with key connections in their field, developing real networks with smart people who do what they want to do, and heeding their wisdom. Money smartly spent on to-the-point skills in schools that target fields with high starting salary averages will get students quickly earning and immersed in their occupation where they can continue seeking mentors. Filling in the gaps with free lectures at Open Course Ware (http://ocw.mit.edu) or Coursera (www.coursera.org) can make a very rounded professional ready to take the world by storm. What kind of training might you add to this unconventional real-life M.B.A. concept?

► What Is the Cost of an Online Degree?

The top online schools from which to earn an MBA are rated by combined rankings from *U.S. News*, *The Economist*, and *Businessweek* as the best in the country for the price.

School	Program Cost	Per-Credit Cost
Carnegie Mellon University Tepper School of Business	$118,080	$615
Indiana University Kelley School of Business	$58,395	$1,145
Arizona State University W.P. Carey School of Business	$53,900	$1,123
University of Florida School of Business	$59,696	$1,244
North Carolina State University Jenkins Graduate School of Business	$53,685	$1,193
Temple University Fox School of Business	$62,208	$1,296
Pennsylvania State University Smeal College of Business	$59,312	$1,235
University of Virginia Darden School of Business	$125,000–$135,000	N/A
University of Maryland Robert H. Smith School of Business	$29,148	$694

Continuing Enrichment and Professional Training for Adults

This arena is very creative and encompasses learning that is as much for enjoyment as it is for occupational enhancement. Many colleges have an adult continuing or enrichment education sector that is sometimes called community ed. You've probably seen community ed catalogs featuring everything from photography and watercolor classes to training on interpersonal skills, relationship counseling, and even flirting. This delivery system is open to most any idea as long as it is fun and non-offensive.

Taking some of what's offered as in-person continuing education and creating a blended learning opportunity might be providing your community with new learning models. Often community centers and continuing ed don't incorporate online learning with other subjects, instead offering online proficiency classes, when doing the former would accomplish two things at once.

While most community ed classes are conducted face-to-face, there is room for creating online tools such as videos, quizzes, and lectures that greatly enhance the experience. This section of the industry may offer the most room for creativity because there are no standardized experiences to be measured against, or pre-designed certificates or degrees.

aha!

Dev Bootcamp, a 10-week training course in programming, costs only $12,200. It takes people with no experience and teaches them how to code. These outcomes are far better than for students fresh out of a M.B.A. programs. In 2012, 88 percent of its graduates got job offers at an average starting salary of $79,000 ("A Smart investor Would Skip the M.B.A." by Dale Stephens, *The Wall Street Journal*, 3/1/13). Brainstorm how your courseware ideas could help learners save money while getting condensed experiences.

Enter-train Them

Aligning yourself with community centers and continuing education branches of colleges helps advertise your product and reach a large audience already interested in self-development, entertainment, meeting new people, or just plain fun. Being an entertainer as well as a teacher—someone who can make sometimes shy people feel welcome—is critical for this area of distance learning. Because people often reach out to enrichment learning as a social function, they are not just looking for information; rather, they seek stimulating exchanges with like-minded people with whom they can possibly build a community, albeit a partially virtual one.

You can, of course, go solo and also receive additional exposure by affiliating in some way with other businesses and organizations, which means you need to have good presentation, networking, and social skills. Giving talks to specialty clubs on your area of expertise is a good way to test the receptiveness of your subject matter on your would-be market and see if you enjoy the interaction that ensues. You can follow talks up with an online module focus group.

Child and Young Adult Education

Distance learning is filling gaps all over this market, such as those to help the Common Core Standards Initiative (CCSI) succeed. The state-led CCSI, developed in 2009, has been adopted by 43 states, the District of Columbia, four territories, and the Department of Defense Education Activity (DoDEA). It uses consistent, real-world learning goals and provides a way for teachers to measure student progress throughout the school year to ensure they are on the pathway to success in their academic careers. This ensures all students, regardless of where they live, are graduating from high school prepared for college, career, and life.

The standards are informed by the best state standards already in existence and the experience of teachers, content experts, states, and leading thinkers. Students are put through the latest retention methods to ensure the information is really sinking in and that they can refer back to the materials using critical thinking and problem-solving skills. Distance educators seeing a great opportunity here are using the latest retention methods in their designs.

Another goal of CCSI is to create a globally competitive U.S. workforce, which brings the opportunity to focus children on the subject matter of other cultures and languages as a must. The "2014 Curriculum of the Future" research report by the Center for Digital Education (www.thecenterdigitaled.com) reveals the drivers of digital education in schools. Some schools, such as those in the Guthrie Common School district in Texas, used an immersive online language program to fulfill state curriculum requirements without hiring more instructors, achieving a 96.4 pass rate and 295 percent increase in active learners.

fun fact ☺

In a recent 12-year study conducted by the Department of Education, students' learning outcomes, (test results) were better with online learning methods than with face-to-face instruction. The report shows that students also earned higher grades overall than those who received face-to-face instruction.

Gamification is a trend that adults and children have made popular by favoring this style of teaching that takes learners through a game of fun challenges, making learning totally absorbing. Creating courseware that combines this style with filling a need makes it extra magnetic.

As new priorities change the structure of traditional education, your key to success lies in creating products that address several needs at once. Keep your eyes on trade journals and research to make sure trends don't shift without you.

Where Do You Fit In?

You, as a future trainer, are a unique combination of experiences and the style with which you convey your knowledge is like a fingerprint—completely original. A large part of what makes distance learning successful is the trainer's ability to address an exact need and convey the material in a way that matches the target audiences' learning style and needs. The best way to address all of these fine points is to create an outline that acts as a guide, identifying the what, how, and why for your teaching plan. Taking an inner inventory of your talents and tendencies can help ensure you structure the right career for your nature.

Multiple Markets, One Concept

You may offer your training services to a combination of these markets, such as the way Carl Tyson, CEO of Thinkwell (www.thinkwell.com), does. Thinkwell, an online video learning specialist that offers global education, has redefined what educators and students think of as a textbook. By studying the benefits of strong mentorship in learning and bridging the access gap between students and dynamic professors, Thinkwell has created distance learning videos that capture the kind of educational leadership that leaves lifetime impressions for the homeschooled and higher education crowds.

If you've ever had a teacher who changed your life and have stopped to wonder why he or she was different from the others, you have something in common with the Thinkwell development team. By using methods that help learners connect the dots of understanding, they have bragging rights to decreased failure rates, including a more than 60 percent increase in passing grades at the University of San Antonio's biology course.

Taking 16 college-level courses and replacing the usually intimidating, massive textbooks that accompany them with online courses make the learning feel like taking a relaxing walk with some very smart friends. It removes some of the stressful barriers to learning. Pre-algebra, calculus, biology, chemistry, and physics are just a few of the courses

Thinkwell has supplied to homeschool students, gifted children, high school and college students, and adult enrichment learners.

Combining great professors with dynamic teaching styles and creating lessons that transport the outer world directly to the student is just part of why the videos are so engaging. Utilizing different teaching methods for a variety of learning styles has been another way the lessons get through to students the way no textbook can.

Build a Unique Product

You also might want to use your skills and interest to build a foundational support product for the eLearning industry, like James Milojkovic, Ph.D. did. He created a two-tiered product that works beautifully to give new and seasoned educators everything they need to teach online without having to understand the technical aspects of software. First, his leadership development and organizational transformation consultancy KnowledgePassion, Inc. (www.knowledgepassion.com) coaches people like you on everything they need to know through video chat. Second, he "co-designed a new, state-of-the art, private membership, video platform called Athena (www.athena.mediacode.net) designed primarily for me to use with my private executive clients at KnowledgePassion and later made available for everyone who wished to showcase and sell their expertise online." Basically, new trainers can just plug their content in and Athena does the rest.

A Realistic Week as an Online Trainer

There are many options for being an online trainer. You may be teaching a subject face-to-face for a university or independently and adding online courses to the mix to enhance what you already offer. You may have an unrelated business that pays your bills and want

▶ Employers Investment Facts

Where do employer dollars go? According to ATD's "2014 State of the Industry Report," they heavily invest in their employees. Here's how it's done:

- ▶ Percent of corporate expenditures spent on internal training: 63
- ▶ Percent spent on external training: 27
- ▶ Percent spent on tuition reimbursement: 10
- ▶ Percent of training delivered with technology: 30

to teach to forward your special interest or hobby, for your own growth and stimulation, in addition to enriching your audience's lives.

What about creating online training services as a way to enhance your current business? PhiPilates (www.phipilates.com) instructors sell webinars, online courses, DVDs, and live workshops to their studio clients. Fitness trainers operating a successful gym or personal training business sometimes generate, as an added perk for their clients, mobile/smartphone apps that give a five-minute workout plan, or new stretching methods. Offering this for free for "gold level" customers or charging a small fee are two options to consider. You could use this idea to attach online learning to your real-life business.

Cadence, Devices, and Audience Goals

How frequently you offer your classes, the density of the information you include, and the devices you choose to convey that education with will be determined by a review of your goals and target audience's wants and goals. Do they wish to increase their earning power with advanced degrees or just look for enrichment or enjoyment? Would they like a three-minute video to watch on their mobile device during breakfast, or are they committed to a few hours a week of absorbing information?

A person's social interests, socioeconomic status, current education level, maturity, drive, values, and sometimes age factor into how they will receive your product. Identifying the range of these factors in your target client will help keep your offerings on track. For example, if you are a personal trainer and want to give your clients a perk with a freebie video while attracting them to a series of videos for which you'd charge money, you might think about making a weekly, 60-second motivational tips piece that would be routed automatically to their phones on Monday mornings. It could have one dynamic exercise that could be performed in a car during rush hour, and two eating healthy on the go tips. By condensing the material you acknowledge the fast-pace lifestyle of your clients, respect their time, and don't spin your wheels making a tool they don't have time to use.

Fill the Need

There are online courses being provided as solutions for things you would never even think of before the other person invented it—but that's the ticket—you need to be the one to think of those "aha!" solutions first. Try looking at this list of business ideas for real challenges, then think of a few of your own. Don't worry about whether they sound outlandish. Brainstorming is about pulling brilliant thoughts from your subconscious and you can't do that if you're feeling inhibited. Just let it all hang out and give it a try.

▶ *First-Aid Training for Pets and Their People.* People love their pets and, yes, there are DVDs available to rent to teach them CPR and other first aid techniques for their buddies, but what if you took it to a whole new level where they could earn certificates and become pretty advanced in their knowledge? This would not replace vet visits. It would enhance the relationship with the vet the same way being well informed before a doctor visit helps us humans.

▶ *Body Simulator.* There are some fun apps out there that let you see what you look like with different hairstyles, and even a way to dress yourself up online like a paper doll, but what if you wanted to see how different workouts might produce different effects on your physique? Do you really want huge quads? Maybe something else would look better. Personal trainers would be interested in this.

▶ *Plastic Surgery Simulator.* Doctors use these in the office but it might be something you could sell to a whole gamut of vanity procedure businesses, such as those who do chemical peels, botox injections, etc.

▶ *How to Get Out of a Gang.* Youth trapped in gang lifestyles just can't seem to get out. The gang provides a family structure the kids crave and take care of all of their needs. A product that works with local law enforcement and youth groups to show kids steps they can take to be safe and get out would help address a huge problem.

▶ *Ending Child Marriage Trainer.* This big movement is underway as aid workers try to reach even the tiniest villages only accessible by foot to educate and enforce the eradication of girls being forced into marriage at as young as nine years old. Training that addresses cultural respect and providing incentives for these communities could help the movement.

▶ *Help Me Write a Book.* Writing the great American novel is a romantic fantasy that remains on a lot of bucket lists. Trouble is, most people don't have the discipline or far-ranging design plans to keep it on target until it's finished. What if you designed a template program that gave the writer daily assignments and plugged them into a book format?

▶ *Interpersonal Relationships Games Simulator.* Wouldn't it be fun to be able to say what you wanted to say to people without regard to what would happen? In long-term relationships people realize the impact of their words and choose them carefully, not wanting to burn bridges. Is it possible for you to design a program that generates an online character based on all the ways a real-life partner has responded to events in the past and will calculate ways they will respond to events in the future? This could be a fun tool for choosing communication choices without fear.

> ▶ *Nutritional Lack Calculator.* Snackers could plug everything they eat into this program and it would tell them what they still need to eat and do to balance out lacking nutrients and needed exercise based on their abilities and food preferences.

> ▶ *The Educated Wine Connoisseur.* Education and enjoyment wine classes that combine tastings at local wine shops, your online tutorial with a comic edge pre-tasting, continuing education, and an earned certificate through edX's World of Wine, From Grape to Glass class (www.edx.org/course/world-wine-grape-glass-adelaid-ex-wine101x-0).

Niche Discovery

There is a new training opportunity every time a new need is identified. If you look at some of the profitable niche training areas in the following list by LearnDash (www.learndash.com), what new ideas do they make you think of? Write down expansions of each of these ideas to get started brainstorming.

Training Industry Profitable Markets

- ▶ Adult and Continuing Education
- ▶ Aeronautics Training
- ▶ Assessment and Testing
- ▶ Authoring Tools
- ▶ Automotive Training
- ▶ Certification Development
- ▶ Certification Training
- ▶ Community Colleges
- ▶ Compliance/Regulatory Training
- ▶ Content Development
- ▶ Continuous Improvement Training
- ▶ Culinary Training School
- ▶ Customer Service Training
- ▶ Customer Training
- ▶ Delivery and Meeting Tools
- ▶ Diversity Training
- ▶ eLearning
- ▶ Energy and Utilities Training

- ▶ Enterprise Architecture Courses
- ▶ Executive Coaching
- ▶ Executive Education
- ▶ Food Service Training
- ▶ Government Policy Training
- ▶ Hospitality Training
- ▶ HR and Occupational Development Courses
- ▶ International Translation Services
- ▶ IT Training
- ▶ Language Training
- ▶ Leadership Training
- ▶ Learning Management System (LMS)/Course (or Content) Maintenance System (CMS)
- ▶ Medical Education
- ▶ MOOCs
- ▶ Online Education
- ▶ Professional Education Programs
- ▶ Project Management Training
- ▶ Quality Control Training
- ▶ Retail Training
- ▶ Safety Training
- ▶ Sales Training
- ▶ Serious Games and Simulations
- ▶ Team Building
- ▶ Training Consulting
- ▶ Training Outsourcing
- ▶ Workforce Development Training

Though it may be challenging to enter a new market, one of the biggest hurdles you may have as a greenhorn in distance education is just staying focused. Opportunities overflow as successful companies try to meet the demand for training while technology and new psychological discoveries about learning merge and emerge. You may have a job creating custom content for a training company or corporation as you build your sample lessons up for your business, or you may create online cooking and nutrition tutorials for a hospital independently and want to expand, but wherever you start, you can be sure it will lead to acquiring new skills and transcending your initial plans. The possibilities are endless.

▶ Top Success Factors for Successful Distance Learning

The International Council on Archives Education and Training, an organization dedicated to archival preservation of the world's heritage through documents, provides a network for educators, trainers, and research professionals to support the exchange of information, preparation of training materials, and record keeping. Its top ten keys to successful distance education are:

1. The trainer needs to be enthusiastic and committed.

2. The team should include good administrative support and, depending in the type of materials and delivery methods used, a good design and production staff.

3. The teaching materials must be properly planned so they are tested and ready in time. Most of the work occurs before the material reaches the students.

4. There must be facilitation and encouragement of learner interaction with both trainer and other learners.

5. The trainer needs to keep in regular contact with all the students.

6. Competent use of any technology used is a prerequisite. It should be fully tested and explained to the students so they are familiar and comfortable with it.

7. Communication and technical problems should be dealt with as they arise.

8. Trainers need to use a variety of methods for interaction and feedback (e.g., one-on-one and conference calls, snail mails, email, video and computer conferencing).

9. Students could keep a diary of their views on progress and course content that they submit or share in some way at frequent intervals.

10. It is crucial to have a residential course at least once, preferably at the beginning, to help learners settle into the distance learning routine and to give some direction on study techniques.

What Kind of Training Will You Offer?

It is only by really studying your market and constantly writing down your ideas in a business journal that you will develop products to serve them. Great ideas are fleeting and the types of training opportunities are boundless. Matching them up isn't so easy, but you don't have to set up shop and work for yourself right away. You could keep your current day job and teach a few subjects part time while you learn the ropes. Are you an expert in a few niche subjects? Training is needed on every subject imaginable. Look at the list below of existing businesses and imagine how they came about. Incorporate that kind of thinking in your business journal, identifying various needs and ideas to fill them.

▶ *The Distance Learning Center for Addiction Studies* (http://dlcas.com) provides the educational training hours needed to either obtain or maintain a credential as a drug/alcohol counseling professional.

▶ *The Church and School of Wicca* (http://wicca.org/courses/basiccourse.html) Ensures, on completion of the courses, that students will have working knowledge of Celtic witchcraft for intellectual and philosophical enlightenment and self-enrichment, or to become practicing witches.

▶ *Funeral Service Education*, Stratford career education (www.scitraining.com/Funeral_Service_Education).

▶ *Peacekeeper Training Courses*, Peace Operations Training Institute Study peace and humanitarian relief any place, any time (www.peaceopstraining.org/courses/).

It is only by truly studying and listening to your potential clients that you can please them, and that should organically lead you to new, expanded ways and places to offer your training. Focus on your taking your first steps in a quality way and how each leads to something new.

Start Your Engines

As with most new businesses, the first two years have the potential to be most challenging as you tackle each new aspect for the first time using precious time just understanding how things work. The first year you'll spend building the foundation of your professional network, getting educated about your industry and competitors, attaining needed certificates and training, and creating your core identity projects that show potential clients who you are. As you build your reputation, you'll need to dedicate time to solving customer service issues, creating policies that leave people happy and are manageable for you, and budgeting hours for projects that come in suddenly, even though you may already be on another job.

Do You Have the Time?

A study by the Association for Talent Development using 47 respondents breaks down development time per finished hour of instruction into many categories. Seventy-one percent of the developers surveyed used Microsoft PowerPoint and Word as their predominant software and Adobe Flash and Captivate were used by 50 percent of respondents. Building hours contributing to the finished hour ranged from 43 to 1,743 depending on a number of factors such as high interactivity with animations, lesson subject matter simulations, and instructor-led vs. text-only instruction. View the complete study results here: www.td.org/Publications/Newsletters/Learning-Circuits/Learning-Circuits-Archives/2009/08/Time-to-Develop-One-Hour-of-Training.

Another useful statistic to project how much time crafting lessons will take is if you already have a "stand-up" or in-person training module, know that you will reduce converting that training into eLearning by an average of 40 to 50 percent, according to Karl M. Kapp, assistant director at Bloomsburg University's Institute for Interactive Technologies.

To develop a realistic forecast of a time budget, you can create your own averages starting now by using a time tracking template, then average your numbers with studies of more advanced work that is most like what you will be doing in the future. Download the template at http://docs.google.com/spreadsheet/ccc?key=0Amna-CF2gnpvdEhaYVZuVn oxSDV4RU92WC1aNkNocWc&usp=sharing#gid=0.

Learn by Doing

Instead of deciding exactly what you're going to offer the hungry masses, it might be prudent to experience some of the moving parts that make the machine run by choosing an entry point and jumping in. You don't have to have your role completely determined. Look at this list of job descriptions or business offerings to see which fits your interest level and skills.

Instructor-Led Online Learning Provider

You create online training that fits your students' schedules, accessing it whenever they like (asynchronously) and/or real time (synchronously) using a mix of complementary technologies. Experience in education and training will serve you well in this role, but you might have to hire additional instructors depending on the magnitude of what you offer. You can also purchase content to use for your lessons. You either have to purchase or create and license your own delivery mechanism to get the lessons smoothly to your students online. As an online school or eLearning center, your finished product is original.

Content Provider

You develop educational material either for yourself or others, which then is packaged and delivered by learning providers. You use software to do this, such as Soft Chalk (www.softchalk.com), CourseLab (www.courselab.com), or Articulate (www.articulate.com), or create your authoring tools. Startup costs for being a content provider can be low depending on what kind of a team and technology you hire to help. A background in education and deep knowledge of several content areas is important, unless you plan on hiring subject matter experts. You need to have a solid understanding of the way buyers like to see this kind of product put together in order to really sell it. Look at these content providers to see how they present themselves:

▶ SweetRush—www.sweetrush.com
▶ Bottom-Line Performance—www.bottomlineperformace.com
▶ Allen Interactions—www.alleninteractions.com

Exam Preparation Site

You provide prep services for several of the most popular higher education and/or industry-specific tests (e.g., food safety, technical certifications, driver's license, etc.). You provide "test run" tests with sample questions students can expect from the real exam, chat rooms or forums for students to discuss related issues and act as study buddies, and resources to related or supporting material. You make your money from student subscriptions and renting ad space on your site. IT workers are a big market for these sites as they have many certifications to prep for. Here are some examples of exam prep services:

▶ The Conference (www.theconferenceonline.org)—The International Conference of Funeral Service Examining Boards NBE Mortuary Science exam
▶ Khan Academy (www.khanacademy.org/test-prep/sat)—SAT exam

▶ Google for Education (www.google.com/edu)—Google Certified Teacher exams

Certification Provider

You provide course training, tests, and certification for any of a variety of industries. Partnering with a large, mature company that can send a lot of traffic your way by frequent recommendations per its website or training materials is mandatory for success in this area. Here are examples:

▶ QC Makeup Academy (www.qcmakeupacademy.com)—Makeup artist (MUA) exam and certification
▶ Google for Education (www.google.com/edu)—Google Certified Teacher
▶ National Cat Groomers Institute of America (www.nationalcatgroomers.com)— Certified Feline Master Groomer (CFMG)

Web Aggregator

You offer endless resources for students to shop for online learning opportunities, screening and reviewing choices to include established learning environments. You research and provide resources for students to compare and contrast organizations against one another, including benefits and price points. Your challenges are to create strong relationships with these institutions to be able to offer partnership deals to students, and to put enough time into informing students of the elements that surround their choices, through blogging or features on your site. Here are some examples:

▶ Online Universities (www.onlineuniversities.com)
▶ Guide to Online Schools (www.guidetoonlineschools.com)
▶ Get Educated (www.geteducated.com)

Reseller and Middleman

Some of the things you do in this role are to provide consulting for distance learning companies, resell courses, customize content, or provide technical assistance or media tools. Here are some examples:

▶ Hol Consulting Services (www.holconsultingservices.com)
▶ Devex (www.devex.com)
▶ Skillsoft (www.skillsoft.com)

Develop Your Courses

Beginning with knowing what your audience goals are creates a mission for your course design to follow. You can refer back to the audience goals to ensure each media tool you choose to convey the education helps the mission, and doesn't create barriers. We cover some of what you need to know about finding out what your audience goals are in Chapter 5, which is all about market research. Here is a guide to creating stimulating lessons for memory retention:

► In analyzing your audience, find out what they already know and set your stage for that. There's no reason to teach under their level and doing so can make attention stray or create irritation.

► Make material relevant to the students by working in a context that is specific to their lives and goals. For example, if you are teaching teens, make sure you are up on the latest tech gadgets, movies, and pop-culture icons, and work those in.

► Use humor as an equalizer and destressor. Use it too much and you'll detract from the material. Use it just enough and with great timing, and it will help learners associate and retain key learning principles.

► Stories or unusual analogies help illustrate points, engage the learner, and plant roots in stages (or chapters of the story) that can help memory retention. Keeping things fun is always a good thing.

► Try to inject a human element to the most digital or virtual parts of your classes by using photographs, illustrations, or recorded human voices.

► Use multimedia sources selectively to texture your message and breathe freshness into your delivery. Some students resonate more with reading text, others by viewing a video, and some are most stimulated by group discussion. Use all of these elements appropriately and you will increase your chances of a strong connection.

► Research college texts and send away for a few that support your material, then read them yourself. It's time consuming but necessary. Once Norma Schuh narrowed her search for textbooks that were perfect for her Confronting Mortality class, she requested copies for review from several publishing companies. They were happy to oblige after confirming that she indeed was part of the adjunct teaching faculty. "Personally reading the text myself, rather than reading about it, assured my satisfaction with the content, writing style, presentation approach, visuals, teaching aids, etc.," says Schuh.

▶ What Is SCORM?

Sharable Content Object Reference Model (SCORM) was produced by a research group sponsored by the United States Department of Defense for its Advanced Distributed Learning (ADL) initiative. It is a technical standard that acts as translator-communicator of sorts and allows learning content and learning management systems (LMSs) that are SCORM conformant to communicate with each other, much in the same way that movies on DVD, no matter where they are from, can all be played on your DVD player.

▶ Use short burst of learning and give learners a chance to test their knowledge, which then reinforces it each time they realize they can use it in context, or answer questions correctly. This is called "chunking."

▶ eLearning Industry's "2015 Instructional Design Trends Compass" report stresses the importance of eliciting emotion. You can do this in all of the efforts listed above and it will help the student become attached to the material and place importance on succeeding.

Building Your Portfolio

Somewhere in this mix, as you either learn on the job or start from scratch building your own company, you'll need to get started building a showcase of your own work: your portfolio. You can use work you've built on a team with others or create some samples with online tools we'll talk about later. Think of your goal as creating a few very strong pieces that show the world what you can do without giving away all of your knowledge. The work should represent your potential and the unique ideas you bring to the table.

Building sample work in the beginning to show potential clients is a little simpler than later on when you'll need a lot of technical assistance. The most potential for edupreneurs lies at the intersection where great ideas for courses meet the technical know-how to make it happen at its highest functioning level. Choosing an LMS that can keep up with the way learners want to learn and your continual product development is important. The best ideas in the world can seem invisible if their presentation isn't understood or is shot through with glitches.

When we asked Carl Tyson about the smartest marketing move Thinkwell has ever made, his answer wasn't technically marketing related. He said, "We went into the business believing that having the best content would win. We quickly learned that in the digital age 'tools' are massively important. The flexibility of the content and the huge amount of content make it critically important to provide tools that allow learners to manage and identify what they need and want. Khan Academy (www.khanacademy.org) is a great example. Students don't need to know anything other than the type of problem they want solved. Khan Academy can take them to an example and work it out of them. Powerful. Instant answers online anytime."

Diane Elkins says, "The issue with LMSs is not that they aren't keeping up with technological advances. It is more that they can be cumbersome to use and companies often can't get the type of information out of them that they want. For example, I have a client who needs to get question-level statistics to help with reporting for grant funding that they received to build the course. My course sends that data to the LMS, but the LMS won't report it at an aggregate level. They can see how Sally or Joe answered each questions, but they can't get a report that says 75 percent of people answered B."

Every professional we talked to agreed that making courseware that is 100 percent functioning for the student with all technical needs accounted for takes much more time than you think it will, and that is why people often form teams. *Learning Solutions* magazine advises, "Once you decide how much time you'll need for your first project, triple it." When we asked Dr. James "Milo" (Milojkovic) what he wishes he had known when he started he said, "It takes way longer than you think reasonable. It takes way more money than you think reasonable. It takes a team of dedicated professionals." Granted, Milo both operates a consulting business (www.knowledgepassion.com) and helps run Athena (www.athena.mediacode.net), but this is still pretty consistent with what the other professionals say, even if their businesses are on a different level.

Diane Elkins talks about the tricky nature of using past work to dazzle future clients, "If you came from a full-time job creating training, your former employer may not let you share what you've done with anyone. Plus, you may have signed a proprietary content and nondisclosure agreement and that can make getting your portfolio started difficult."

fun fact ☺

What is an edupreneur? First defined by authors Dr. Don Leisey and Charles Lavaroni of *The Educational Entrepreneur: Making a Difference* as: "a person within the public schools who takes hands-on responsibility in creating and developing a program, product, service, and/or technology for the enhancement of learning consistent with the stated goals of and supported by that organization." The meaning has morphed to encompass a greater umbrella of educators as expressed by *Edtech Digest* as "an entrepreneur in the education sector."

Choosing an LMS

The LMS is a software platform that delivers, manages, and tracks results and generates reports for online courses and training programs that can be hosted in the cloud, remotely, or on local servers. There are many LMSs to choose from as online learning explodes, but here are some popular ones:

tip

Kickstart your online training skills with an array of low-cost and free classes like these on edX. org: Creating a Course with edX Studio, edX or Design and Development of Games for Learning, MITx.

- ▶ Moodle (www.moodle.com)
- ▶ Edmodo (www.edmodo.com)
- ▶ Blackboard (www.blackboard.com)
- ▶ SumTotal Systems (www.sumtotalsystems.com)
- ▶ Skillsoft (www.skillsoft.com)
- ▶ Cornerstone OnDemand (www.cornerstoneondemand.com)
- ▶ Brightspace (www.brightspace.com)

In Chapter 8 we'll talk more about how to choose the right one for your business.

Work with Nonprofits

Building great pieces over years only to realize they are locked for viewing can be pretty frustrating. There are ways around this problem. The first is to focus on work that the client will want to expose as much as possible. You want to be able to display snippets or short demos of work on your website. "We work with a lot of nonprofits and they are comfortable with me showing the projects I created for them because it gets the word out about their mission. Other clients resell the products I create for them so they want that exposure. Sometimes, even if the material is sensitive and you think the client would not want to let you display it, all you have to do is ask and they may let you if you remove their logo or branding from the project," Diane Elkins says.

Several of the trainers we interviewed suggested doing projects with nonprofits to build your portfolio. This way your work is almost always shared and it is sometimes easier to get these jobs (for a lower hire rate) because nonprofit budgets aren't usually big and after all, you're new, so your rates are probably well matched.

Build Classes Today

Try using one of the free LMSs that will allow you to build courses, utilize mobile interface design techniques, create games and quizzes, design and control your own private LMS, and allow for usability with popular course management systems (CMS) such as Blackboard. Eliademy (www.eliademy.com) and Course Sites by Blackboard (www.coursesites.com) are just two of many.

Harness Your Course for Growth

Choosing one course to develop completely and sell at the same time could help fund parts of your business growth. In a recent *Forbes* article, instructors that were surveyed on Udemy (www.udemy.com), a popular teaching platform, made an average of $7,000 annually with their courses, which often only run 30 minutes. A recent sampling of courses showed a cost range from $47 to $197. Udemy also offers free courses and has a lot of traffic. The basic message about selling your courses on Academy of Mine (www.academyofmine.com),

aha!

Get connected to your next nonprofit job with Non Profit Connect (www.npconnect.org), which helps match professionals to nonprofits seeking services. Designing training for a nonprofit as a donation can plump up your resume and be a good way to get exposure, as the group will be happy to sing your praises on their site.

another LMS, is that there is little or no immediate payoff to creating an ecourse from scratch, however, in increments traffic and sales increase steadily. Just like with any other promotional campaign, these sites are controlled by the same psychology: People need to see something over and over for it to sink in and one day they choose it after months of exposure. This is, of course, only a valid statement if you choose an LMS that does promotion well. Watching the traffic pick-up with different eduprenuers on Academy of Mine went like this: ". . . the first month of traffic saw 128 visitors, the next month saw a jump to 552. Still, a very small amount of traffic, but it's a 331 percent increase in traffic which, if you look at it that way, is a huge jump! And the next month we're over 1,000 visitors and shortly after that we're just under 4,000/month," according to *Forbes*.

You can sell your courses through third-party platforms, sell eLearning materials to teachers, or sell them from your own site. Here are some examples of places to sell your work.

Third-Party Platforms

▶ www.opensesame.com
▶ www.lynda.com/default.aspx
▶ http://elearningmarketplace.com
▶ www.shopify.com

eLearning Materials for Teachers

► www.teacherspayteachers.com
► www.sharemylesson.com

Open Schedule Online Courses

With open schedule online courses, students are allotted the greatest amount of freedom. This is an asynchronous form of learning in which students are provided internet-based textbooks, mailing lists, email, and bulletin boards to complete their coursework. At the beginning of classes, students are provided a set of deadlines, but are allowed to work at their own pace as long as the work is turned in by the deadline. This type of learning is great for students who work well independently and do not procrastinate.

Hybrid Distance Learning

Hybrid courses combine synchronous and asynchronous learning to create a structure in which the student is required to meet at a specific time in a classroom or internet chat room. However, they are allowed to complete assignments on their own time and may pass them in through an online forum. This option is sometimes offered when a university lacks adequate space to accommodate all its courses.

Computer-Based Distance Learning

The main difference between computer-based learning and hybrid learning is that students are not allowed an open schedule. They are required to meet in a specific computer lab or in a classroom at a designated time each week.

Fixed-Time Online Courses

The most common type of distance learning today is fixed-time courses. As the title states, these courses are strictly online, but students are required to login to their online learning site at a specific time. Although they are completely online, the format remains synchronous because mandatory live chats are often required.

Promotion and Organization of Your Work

After you've created your first few pieces and have a solid understanding of what each person on an "eduteam" does, it's time to think about putting together a course catalog. In developing this you learn a lot about what your product does and does not do, and how the public should perceive it. Writing out a succinct summary of what your course offers includes information such as the benefits students will earn after taking it, what program of interest it falls into and how it supports that department (if you are teaching for a larger institution such as DeVry, Kaplan, or Walden), and degree, accreditation or certificate availability. You want to clearly represent the type of course it is as well, because students choose partially by the style in which they best learn. For example, is it a seminar with heavy interactive web modules, or is it a webinar series culminating with a final in-person, interactive debate?

Landing Pages

You'll create a landing page for each affiliate or university site you are listed on. Using fitting keywords in your descriptions will help students find your courses. Make a list of every single way someone could search for your class online and use those words in your description. Not sure? Look up classes similar to yours and read some descriptions on Petersons.com, a popular host site for top schools. You can search there by degree, areas of study, tuition, and location. When you click on a description for the online school choices, you see with a certain area of study that the style of learning is somewhat defined. Whether there are online chat, mobile apps, online office hours, digital textbooks, and transfer credits accepted are some of the features covered. These are things to include in your own descriptions.

If you design your course page for display on sites of different institution, make sure the look and copy is consistent, allowing for relevant changes per the host or affiliate. You want to make it as easy as possible for people to find you.

If you have your own website, you want to also list on it the participating schools that also feature your work. You might create a landing page such as the type used by retailers on Amazon.com, showing off some of the more interesting features of your class, the same way that the "Look Inside" feature allows viewers to read a sample portion of books on Amazon.

The structure of the catalog on your website and affiliate landing pages should stay simple and read as comprehensive but not overwhelming. If you are offering degrees or certification, link those to an explanation of what is required to complete the degree, and what types or versions of that particular degree are available.

Your Bio Presence

Whether you've got a master's degree in education and want to teach MBA classes, or have been working as a carnival ride operator and want to teach amusement park

► Where Does the Time Go?

Look at the list below to see how trainers spend their time:

- ► Writing custom content
- ► Meeting with subject-matter experts
- ► Meeting with designers
- ► Learning new software and apps
- ► Hiring talent, building a team
- ► Client consultations
- ► Client, demos, presentations, and showcasing
- ► Client meetings for product development
- ► Training corporate employees on-site
- ► Conducting seminars and giving talks
- ► Chatting with students about assignments
- ► Grading assignments
- ► Getting to know new learners
- ► Attending to daily business tasks such as paying bills, accounting, phone and online video/phone calls
- ► Traveling to client locations
- ► Training to become a better trainer
- ► Training to create new products
- ► Networking events, in persons and online
- ► Networking functions and maintenance, such as using LinkedIn, Twitter, and Facebook
- ► Blogging for self and others
- ► Generating ideas for new products

industry safety training, highlighting the experience you have pertinent to your product is mandatory. Your bio presence should exist on LinkedIn and your website and blog, and you should occasionally at least blog about your area of expertise to fortify that presence.

▶ **The Four Points of the Square**

The success of your new adventure will depend on accounting for and completely developing these factors:

▶ *Curriculum*: What will it be? What will it teach and why?

▶ *Students*: Who are they and why do they need or want your courses?

▶ *Marketing*: It won't sell itself, so create a well-thought-out way to tell the world.

▶ *Technology*: How will you travel, communicate, and run your business online?

Establishing your foundation by planning for these elements will help you understand if you need to hire instructors, IT or other experts, and how much to charge for what you produce.

Professional Research

That's on you. You are on your way to becoming an authority, someone other people turn to for advice on how it's done. This means you have to love what you do and consider each day that you learn something new about your mission a gift. Countless researchers, librarians, educators, historians, writers, activists, revolutionaries, archivists, scientists, and swamis have dedicated their lives to discovering and preserving knowledge so that it is there for people like you to uncover. They do this because they understand why knowledge is power and how it can change lives and the world. To be fully committed to your craft is to be fully immersed in all of the available knowledge and research around it. So take advantage of white papers, studies, blogs, trade association social functions, seminars, and anything you can get your knowledge-hungry little hands on to be the best you can be. It's contagious and will show in your product.

Setting Your Rates

You'll need to assign a dollar value to what you do and that starts by figuring out how many hours it takes to make a product and what you can sell it for, or what the market will bear. Diane Elkins says the hourly rate range for contracting professionals who build courses is $25 to $125, with most people falling in the $40 to $70 range. You'll read about how many hours it takes to create one hour of finished product in the study by the Chapman Alliance in Chapter 6, and develop your own averages after you build your first lessons. You'll factor into all of that the rate that your competition is selling work for. If you work with a university or other educational organization, there will be restrictions on what the course is sold for. You'll either be paid a percentage of that per enrollment numbers or just a flat fee. But if you sell your own work, it's easy to set prices just by comparing the most popular similar courses. If you are tempted to seriously undercut the competition with ridiculously low prices, remember that using coupons to get the ball rolling and other free promos need to be figured into the grand scheme of your pricing, as well as the perceived value (or lack thereof) of an inexpensive product. You can also make your money not from the course itself, but from certifying learners. Coursera (www.coursera.org) classes are often free or low cost, but to earn certification learners must pay $49 and up.

Look at the classes on these sites to find some like yours and compare pricing:

▶ *Lynda.com*. Subscription-based video tutorial library with over 80,000 titles of media-skills focused classes. $25 per month to take whatever you like. Includes mobile apps.

▶ *Udemy.com*. Averages 800 new courses per month. Costs range from $10 to $500 with the most popular tech classes averaging around $100.

▶ *Udacity.com*. This tech-focused platform allows users to pay by the month for their education and stop paying if they quit. Classes average $200 per month with certification included.

▶ *Khanacademy.org*. Free micro-video lessons focusing on academic subjects. Learners earn completion badges.

▶ *Skillshare.com*. This emporium of creative classes focuses on visual arts. Join for free for access to a limited number of free classes or join for $10 per month for unlimited access. Membership proceeds help pay teachers.

Going Public

Hosted learning management systems are widely used for education and training purposes and are also great for selling courses. LMSs offer multifunctional learning opportunities and you will be freed from managing the content manually. The LMS will do everything for you.

Sell Courses from Your Own Website

Building your own website and installing an LMS on it is another opportunity. This will let you keep your money, but the investment is higher than letting someone else host your lessons, and building a website from scratch requires some level of expertise. Content management systems like Joomla!, WordPress, and Drupal are quite popular solutions. The platforms are free to install.

Barriers to entry can be low enough to just begin with creating one's own website with a low-cost service and setting up the accompanying ecommerce PayPal add-ons if you are only using your website to create a presence and using LMSs to run your lessons.

You'll need some basic software and only you can decide which fits your needs. If you are working with an organization or with a school, it will usually provide all of the software and systems you need, along with access to technical assistance to get you started.

You can start training on your topic of expertise with no certification or accreditation, if you choose, but getting clients to care about your work starts with illuminating who you are in the most professional way, and getting certified as a trainer looks great on your website.

▶ A Salary Sampling of eLearning Pros

Here is a sampling of salaries in the eLearning industry determined by location and experience. It is calculated by the 2014 eLearning Guild's Research Salary Calculator, which can help you determine your rates. View more at: www.learningsolutionsmag.com/articles/1352/

Title	Location	Experience	Years on Job	Salary
Instructional designer	California	Associate's degree	2	$68,592
Writer	Kentucky	Master's degree	6	$53,595
Content author	Utah	Bachelor's degree	4	$43,570
Creative director	Wisconsin	Bachelor's degree	12	$85,720
Media producer	Florida	Associate's degree	5	$66,461
Planner strategist	Arizona	Doctorate degree	8	$111,452
Information technologist	Illinois	Bachelor's degree	3	$74,591

Barriers to entry can also be high in that there is a lot of competition for personal and corporate allotted training funds. Making sure there is a need where you offer your service and that you've built a strong team and network can increase your potential for success.

Get Certified

Getting additional certifications and degrees in your field never hurts and with online training you could have a very attractive bio in less than a year by taking free courses and investing in a few certifications like those offered at the Association for Talent Development. Its senior manager of communications Kristen Fyfe-Mills says,

> "ATD is the professional association for those who develop talent in the workplace. So, to the degree that an individual pursues this work, we have abundant resources to help them. The common name for many in this profession is 'trainer' and many people who end up in that role get there accidentally. They may have expertise in a particular area and are asked to step in and teach others about what they know.
>
> "There really isn't a direct path to teaching online. Many companies use online training courses to advance [their employees'] knowledge and skills . . . and those who facilitate such training often translate this experience into their own business. Online courses are often offered as a way to efficiently deliver learning in the workplace. Colleges do the same thing.
>
> "ATD offers the only certification for people in the training space. It's called the Certified Professional in Learning and Performance (CPLP) credential. This is a professional certification—it's not an accreditation affiliated with higher education entities. ATD's education and professional development courses are not accredited by any organization. Some institutions of higher education recognize professional experience and certifications as meriting credit, but we don't have any exposure to that, nor do we try to influence those decisions.
>
> "ATD provides countless resources for people who are in the learning and development space. With more than 70 education offerings, blogs, books, and the award-winning TD magazine, we strive to provide professionals in this field with relevant resources that help them do their jobs better. Instructional designers, course writers, and programmers are all roles that exist in the eLearning field. We have resources for all of these roles. We also have a tool called the Career Navigator that allows members to craft a professional development path with our content-based on where they currently are in their careers and where they want to go. Note that Career Navigator is for members."

Additionally, you may know your field and subject matter, but getting top-notch training on how to convey that is important. So many changes in the way students receive information are occurring as new research is done and results are seen with how students respond to new technologies.

Hire Instructors

You may need to hire instructors to help create your product and provide them with the hardware and software they need to do their jobs. The traditional academic model uses instructors with Ph.D.s, but more business-oriented institutions such as the University of Phoenix Online tend to take real-life, on-the-job experience as a serious credential. Depending on your subject matter, you'll have to decide if an academia professional or a business professional holds more credit.

Here are some of the qualifications, titles, and backgrounds the entrepreneurs in this book have harnessed to their advantage:

▶ *Kristen Fyfe-Mills*, an award-winning strategic communicator with experience in nonprofit and corporate communications, broadcasting, advertising, and print journalism, serves as the Association for Talent Development's (ATD) senior communications manager. Her qualifications include a Bachelor of Science in Speech and a Master of Science in Journalism from Northwestern University. She is a certified member of the John Maxwell Team of Coaches, Trainers, and Speakers and she has a Coaching Certificate, ATD.

▶ *Norma Schuh* is an adjunct instructor in the Human Development Graduate Program at St. Mary's University in Minneapolis. Her qualifications include a Bachelor of Science in Secondary Education from Oakland University in Rochester, Michigan, and a Master of Science in Human Development from St. Mary's University in Minneapolis, Minnesota. She is also an author, columnist, playwright, and actress.

▶ *Julie Dirksen* is an independent consultant and instructional designer with more than 15 years of experience creating highly interactive eLearning experiences for clients from *Fortune* 500 companies and technology startups to grant-funded research initiatives. She has a degree in Instructional Systems Technology, a breadth of experience in UX design, game-based learning, and behavior change. She is also an adjunct faculty member in the Visualization Department at the Minneapolis College of Art and Design, where she created and taught courses in project management, instructional design, and cognitive psychology.

▶ *Diane Elkins* is the president and co-founder of Artisan E-Learning, a custom eLearning development company specializing in the use of Articulate Studio, Storyline, Captivate, and Lectora. She is a national eLearning expert and national conference speaker for the E-Learning Guild and the Association for Talent Development (ATD). She is the co-author of the E-Learning Uncovered series, which includes books on Storyline, Studio, Lectora, and Captivate.

tip

If you're a corporate training expert and want to target your marketing toward larger companies because you think their training budgets are bigger, think again. It may be just as profitable to target smaller companies with less than 500 employees. ATD's State of the Industry report shows that smaller organizations spent an average of $1,888 in training per employee compared to larger ones who only spent $838 per employee. The tricky part of the equation is that the larger organizations actually conducted more training hours (36) than the smaller organizations (27).

When Norma Schuh began teaching workshops on aging and mortality, her focus was on helping midlife people face their advancing years in order to live more mindfully and vitally. She'd earned a Master's in Human Development in 2004 from St. Mary's University in Minneapolis, Minnesota and quickly parlayed her wisdom into classes that would guide others to confront the transition to "middlessence" and beyond, while celebrating this unique life juncture.

Teaching online came as a bit of an accident. "I love my subject matter and wanted to share my knowledge at the university level. I approached the same [university] from which I earned my masters to propose a course on personal mortality."

It's important to analyze the current class offerings where you will be teaching in order to define how yours are different or will fill a gap. At first there was some confusion about the need that would be filled in the curriculum by adding Schuh's course. "The university already offered classes on grief and loss, which provide support and training for dealing with the deaths of others. However, my course is about confronting one's own death and recognizing the urgency of living life intentionally and congruently in the finite time we each have." Schuh says.

Ultimately, Schuh's efforts to differentiate her unique material and learning objectives from existing offerings won her course a spot in the curriculum, with the caveat that it would be delivered online to preclude any potential duplication.

Make
It
Official

N ow that you're on your way to developing a
great product and putting together a team of
educational experts, it's time to get create your
business structure, public identity, and get your legal
ducks in a row. In this chapter we'll coach you on creating your mission statement, structuring your business,
and coming up with a fitting business name. You'll read

about which accreditations and certifications to consider adding to your reputation and how to secure legal and financial services to make your debut.

Group Benefits Last a Lifetime

Lining up a number of professionals you can rely on for support will help you move toward your goals. One of the advantages to working within an association or educational institution is the expertise you can draw on from being part of the group. If you're starting from scratch, you can look for guidance from your trade associations, networking groups, and colleagues.

Purchasing a professional membership from a guild such as ATD gives you support and guidance from the built-in bevy of professionals around you. Both Diane Elkins and Julie Dirksen have remained active with their local branches of ATD and eLearning Guild, taking and teaching seminars, attending conferences, and keeping social alliances nurtured. This can connect you with everyone you need for your team.

You can also take advantage of your association with any CMS you may use for technical needs. For example, if you use Joomla! (www.joomla.org) to build your website or use its applications, you will have access to a leadership team that can either point you toward what you need to know or refer you to sources for building a network of advisors.

The Department of Health and Human Services has a mentorship program expressly developed to retain a diverse, high-performance workforce and preserve the knowledge and skills of employees nearing retirement age. Read more about it here: www.mentoring.hhs.gov.

Your Mission

Your mission statement is more than a sentence or two about what you want to do. It serves as a framework and reminder of your specific goals to keep you on track and help you make decisions down the road that might seem confusing. For example, when faced with a potential new business opportunity that feels somewhat out of the realm of your comfort level, you can look at your mission statement and ask yourself if accepting the job will work toward the mission. If it doesn't, you might have some soul searching to do.

Carl Tyson's mission for Thinkwell is "To bring the greatest teachers in the world to large numbers of students in higher education via the Web." This describes his product very well: a video series that replaces textbooks using dynamic professors as hosts conducting conceptual demonstrations in a variety of locations.

Distance trainers get involved in presenting a number of on-site training sessions as part of their marketing plan or curriculum. These can lead to invitations for speaking engagements and other wonderful exposure opportunities. If Carl were to be asked to teach an on-site, ten-session version of one of his current courses to junior high students, he'd look at his mission statement and have to come up with a good reason to move outside it, as that project would; it is not directly geared toward the higher education crowd, or distance led, and it's a long commitment that would pull him away from his mission. It's not mandatory that you only provide the kind of service that supports your mission statement, but it's smart to have most of what you do apply to it. If you start offering a mishmash of varied services, you cloud your time with tasks that don't support your goals and fill your dance card with distractions that could make you miss connecting with work that accomplishes your mission.

Constructing your mission should come from your heart and soul. It should reflect what you most want to spend your time on, because you'll hopefully be expertly doing it for years. It consists of a few sentences, or a paragraph, that defines what you offer, to whom, and what your goal is. It should capture specifics in a short communication style and leave no doubt as to exactly the kind of business you are.

It should appeal to the array of customer types you intend to serve and potential investors in your startup or long-term funding by conveying your enthusiasm and intent. Here are some mission statements from eLearning educators for you to study:

▶ *Palm Beach State College* (www.palmbeachstate.edu). "To provide students an opportunity to learn in an environment which best meets their varied lifestyles, offering credit and noncredit courses, degrees and certifications by distance learning in order to provide opportunities for students that can't attend traditional courses to complete their education remotely."

▶ *College of the Canyons* (www.canyons.edu). "To develop and deliver universally accessible, academically sound, and technologically advanced instruction at a distance, while supporting student success, responding to community needs and promoting faculty innovation."

Answer the questions definitively in Figure 4–1: Mission Statement Worksheet on page 56 to get started creating yours. Be clear and specific. If you need some help defining and translating your ideas into a statement, think about what your product is not, who it will not appeal to, and why:

Julie Dirksen describes her mission statement for Usable Learning as more of an objective: "To apply my extensive instructional design experience and problem-solving skills to the task of improving people's knowledge, work, and lives." This is broad, which allows her to stay on target with her mission while delivering it in several ways, to varied audiences. She is an independent consultant and instructional designer who creates

Mission Statement Worksheet

To develop an effective mission statement, answer these questions:

1. What products and/or services do we produce or offer? _____

    _____

    _____

2. In what geographical location do we operate? _____

    _____

    _____

3. Why does our company exist? _____

    _____

    _____

4. What are our strengths, weaknesses, opportunities, and threats? _____

    _____

    _____

5. Who are our customers? Define the demographic in detail. _____

    _____

    _____

6. What is the unique value of our product and service model? _____

    _____

    _____

7. What gap in the market does our product fill? _____

    _____

    _____

    _____

FIGURE 4–1: **Mission Statement Worksheet**

Mission Statement Worksheet, continued

8. Considering the above, along with our expertise and resources, what business should we be in? _____

   _____

   _____

   _____

   _____

9. What is important to us? What do we stand for? _____

   _____

   _____

   _____

   _____

   _____

10. How do we want people to think of us? _____

    _____

    _____

    _____

    _____

11. Are these answers clear enough to keep our company on track? _____

    _____

    _____

    _____

    _____

    _____

FIGURE 4–1: **Mission Statement Worksheet,** continued

highly interactive eLearning experiences for clients ranging from *Fortune* 500 companies to innovative technology startups to major grant-funded research initiatives. Her focus has been on utilizing the disciplines of educational psychology, neuroscience, change management, and persuasive technology to promote and support the improvement of lives through sustainable, long-term learning and behavioral change. Her delivery system takes many forms; speaking engagements; authoring books; creating and leading online courses; conducting webinars; and consulting.

Diane Elkins' mission statement for Artisan E-Learning is, "We create custom learning experiences by partnering with our clients to craft their perfect solution."

This is also a broad, somewhat open-ended mission statement, that allows for the complete selection of services and broad client base Artisan E-Learning appeals to. Elkins offers an all-inclusive distance learning package to corporations, nonprofits, and government agencies, including self-paced, custom course development, and consulting and training services. That is Elkin's "perfect solution" so clients don't have to go elsewhere to complete the package.

After you've written your mission statement, give it a probationary period. Ask clients if they feel it expresses what they were looking for when they found you, and what they got. When you're sure it's the right fit, you're ready to put it on your website and promotional/marketing materials.

Legal Eagles

To ensure that you get off on the right foot, hire an attorney with startup expertise who can give you advice to grow on. You can use his or her knowledge of the pros and cons of each business structure to determine which one is best for your venture. You can get insight into your lease, buy-sell agreements, licenses, ordinances, bonding, zoning, financing, and human resource hurdles. An experienced business lawyer can minimize your exposure to IRS, occupational, employment, and safety problems. Don't wait until the last minute to line up competent legal counsel you trust. You don't want to put your fate into the hands of a total stranger.

You can reduce the amount of professional fees you have to pay by doing some homework—researching the answers to questions, making some decisions, and knowing how to do part of the paperwork yourself. There's a growing number of books on the subject of forming your own business available from Nolo Press in Berkeley, California, and Simon & Schuster in New York City; also check out Entrepreneur Press's *Start Your Own Business, 6th Edition*. Write or call the Small Business Development Center nearest you, and visit your local library or bookstore for some of the publications listed in the Appendix.

For new edupreneurs, Carl Tyson stresses the importance of "recognizing that a good lawyer is essential for their own protection; and they need to realize that who they take money from as investment is more important than how much money or valuation is offered. It is critical that investors and business people understand the goals and rules of the road as they move forward to build something. Most important, I think, is that the person starting a business needs to have a carefully balanced relationship between their vision and reacting to new information. It is great to have a vision and passion but there will be curves in the road and new information may require flexibility. Also, it is vitally important to build a team of people who work together well. I have made the mistake of hanging on to a really talented person who did good work but could not mesh with the team. Sooner or later that will hurt the entire project. That said, I'd rather stick with someone too long than move too quickly. It's not easy."

Education-Specific Legal Obligations

Making your courseware equally accessible to everyone is your obligation, the same way a restaurant makes entrance into its establishment wheelchair accessible. Everyone must have the right to your services without barriers and while it is not your obligation to cater to every known barrier, there are some rules that are clearly important. In "Distance Education Report" Deborah Brown, associate vice president for legal affairs and human resources, and Ellen Podgor, associate dean of faculty development and distance education, at the Stetson University College of Law outlined several areas distance educators need to be mindful of:

▶ Providing a notice on your site acknowledging you are aware of your obligation to reasonably accommodate those with disabilities. Large font texts for the visually impaired or closed captioning for the hearing impaired are examples of this.

▶ Selecting in-person test sites that are accessible to those with disabilities, if in-person testing is part of your curriculum.

▶ Making sure IT staff managing and creating your site are trained in and aware of the need to provide reasonable accommodations in design and usability.

▶ Understanding both the Rehabilitation Act of 1973 and the Americans with Disabilities Act to avoid having to retroactively make changes to your company policies, business plans, and courseware designs. Check with your state to see if you are obligated to fulfill additional requirements.

▶ Being aware when reviewing and deciding to enter into a technology contract. Choosing a long-term technology company to partner with is a choice that must weather changes such as changing operating locations due to natural disaster or other reasons, how painful it will be if you have to cancel the agreement, how the techs will honor your request to not use your logo or theirs, or vice versa on affiliate sites.

▶ If you are teaching for an accrediting institution, honoring the distance guideline standards set forth in your contract.

For a greater awareness of what legal distinctions distance educators must be aware of, read "Best Practices for Electronically Offered Degree and Certificate Programs" at: http://sacscoc.org/pdf/commadap.pdf.

warning

Images aren't free. You'll need clipart, graphics, video, and photography to make your courses come alive, but don't make the mistake of using material you don't have rights to. There are lots of places to purchase stock material to spice up your concepts, such as at eLearning Brothers (elearningbrothers.com), which sells packages of cutout people images, eLearning templates, audio, video, design coaching, and all kinds of other neat tools to make your work shine.

Forming a Business Entity

Forming a business entity is a big step with long-term consequences. While it is possible to change the legal structure any time in your company's life, it is time-consuming and costly. Converting from a partnership to a C corporation or limited liability company will pose few problems, as will switching from a sole proprietorship or partnership to an LLC. Converting from a C corporation to a partnership, sole proprietorship, or LLC, however—or getting in and out of an S corporation—is more complicated. Think carefully before you finalize your business structure. To ward off impatience and other pressures, look at the three- and five-year projections you put in your business plan to help you stay on course.

If you're like most online learning specialists, you will open as a sole proprietorship or C corporation. There are no special steps required other than obtaining a business license. You may need to file a notice of a fictitious firm name and present it to your bank to open a business account, but there's not a lot more required for you to start selling your products or services.

A partnership is formed through an oral or a written agreement, but a written agreement is advisable. To form a limited liability company, you need to file articles of organization with the state. A separate document, the operating agreement, outlines the rules for managing the firm. A lawyer will charge you about $1,200 to $3,000 for filling out the paperwork. Forming a corporation usually costs between $500 and $2,000 upfront, according to Fred S. Steingold, author of *Legal Guide for Starting and Running a Small Business* (Nolo Press). There is a substantial amount of paperwork involved, including filing articles of incorporation and paying a state filing fee, which varies from $100 to $150.

What's in a Name?

Everything. Your name, like your mission statement, should give a quick impression of what you do. It can be catchy and abstract, but not so much that it sends clients off in another direction entirely. The sound of the word should sound like what your company does. If your branding and product are clean and simple, don't choose an involved name with lots of syllables.

Brainstorm Your Name

Get a thesaurus (or go to www.thesuarus.com), a piece of paper and pen and write:

1. Ten adjectives that describe your company
2. How learners might feel after working with your product
3. A list of words that represent the separate components that make up your product
4. How the world, or your students, will be changed or benefit as a result of taking your courses

Now open that thesaurus and make a list of synonyms for each word you've written down. Try making two columns with the words and putting combinations of two together, or halving two words to make one new word. The brain stimulation company called Lumosity uses parts of words for a specific effect. "Luminosity" means the brightest light a star or galaxy can give off and its root, "lumens" is a measure of the total amount of visible light emitted from a source. This is a perfect example of how an elegant twist on a powerful word can nicely represent your product.

Below are some examples of how to combine words. Try to mix and match your list of synonyms this way in Figure 4–2: Business Name Worksheet on page 63. For example:

tip

There is little paperwork involved in setting up a sole proprietorship. Get the necessary selling permits and other licenses, and notify the city, county, or state of your intention to do business under an assumed name (dba). You pay taxes on the business income as if it were personal salary and assume full liability for anything that goes wrong. You also pay self-employment tax for Social Security and Medicare coverage.

Cloud	+	Scholar	=	Cloud Scholar
Brilliant	+	Teen	=	Brillanteen
Know	+	Instant Access	=	Know Now
Sky	+	College	=	Sky College
Informed	+	Developed	=	Develoform
Academic	+	Wisdom	=	Wisdemic

Why not Wizedemic? Sometimes businesses purposely use an incorrect spelling for their name, which in an industry of literates, is not such a good idea.

Here are some more examples and key words you might consider:

School	+	Journey	=	School Cruise

Scholar	Whiz	Excel	Gray Matter
Pupil	Advance	Intelligence	
Extensive	Wizard	Inclusive	
Smarts	Library	Precocity	

Carl Tyson joined Thinkwell about a year after the founders, brothers, Dan and Chip Heath, and Amy Bryant, created it. "They tossed around a lot of ideas. The one that almost won was Profopolis, which means 'a city of teachers.'" Not sure who came up with Thinkwell, but I love the name and it has served us well."

Protect Your Name

Corporations must register their corporate names with the secretary of state, state Department of Corporations, or commissioner of corporations. Each state's laws on this are a little different. But in every state, you must get permission to use your trade name before incorporation. You have to select a permissible name, make sure it's distinguishable from any corporate name already registered in the state, and then send in an application (with a fee) to reserve the legal right to use that name to identify your business.

Any person who uses a trade name other than his or her surname or any organization that goes by a name other than the last names of the owners must register the name with the state or county as a fictitious business name. This usually means filing a certificate with the county clerk stating who is doing business under that trade name. This is called a dba (doing business as).

If your state has no central fictitious name registration, you may want to check more than one county's records to see if anyone else in your state is using the name you propose for your business. Otherwise, several businesses might use the same name in your state, and if you want to expand your operation, you may run into difficulties.

Business Name Worksheet

List three (or more) variations using your own name for your business:

1. _____

2. _____

3. _____

List three business name ideas associated with your specialty or niche as an eLearning provider:

1. _____

2. _____

3. _____

List three business name ideas associated with your geographic area. You can use the name of your town, county, or state. Or use something that your area is well known for, such as a southwestern region or pristine beaches.

1. _____

2. _____

3. _____

Once you've narrowed it down to one or two choices, take the following steps:

▶ Write it down to see how it looks.

▶ Say it out loud to hear how it sounds.

▶ Check the first initials of each word to ensure the acronym isn't something inappropriate.

▶ Run it by family and friends to see if they are as enthusiastic as you are.

▶ Look in the Yellow Pages and on the web to see if someone else is using it.

▶ Call the county clerk or secretary of state's office to make arrangements for filing it.

FIGURE 4–2: **Business Name Worksheet**

▶ A Name to Remember

Using your own name can get tricky. Alcon, Ward and Partners, Inc. changed its name to Artisan E-Learning. It's possible to lose the rights to branding with your own name, if you're not careful, or it can get complicated if you keep adding talent to your group.

Your name is the cornerstone of your brand, and the identity of your company is a major component of your success. Because image is such an important part of marketing, a lot is riding on your name. Your signage, business cards, name tags, uniforms, vehicles, word-of-mouth advertising, private-label lines, and website will depend on the integrity of your name, so you'll want to guard it carefully.

Separate from the state law issue is the question of whether or not your name has any trademark value because it distinguishes your goods or services from those of other companies. If so, you can register the name for federal trademark protection, which entitles you to stop others from adopting or using it. You must complete a registration form from the U.S. Patent and Trademark Office in Washington, DC.

There are two very different contexts in which your business's name may be used. One is the formal name of your business for purposes of bank accounts, creditors, and potential lawsuits. The second is the name you use to market your goods or services (trademark or service mark). Whether someone is using the same trade name as yours is of less practical importance than if they were using the same trademark, or using the same trade name as a trademark as well. If your corporate name figures into your future marketing plans, you must search for use of the name as a trademark in addition to complying with the corporate name registration requirements. If someone else is the first to use your name as a mark, it doesn't make any difference whether you or they have

save

Ethics and the Law on the Electronic Frontier, a class offered for free by MIT, considers the interaction between law, policy, privacy, transparency, and technology on the internet through these topics:

▶ Legal Background for Regulation of the Internet

▶ Fourth Amendment Law and Electronic Surveillance

▶ Profiling, Data Mining, and the U.S.A. PATRIOT Act

▶ Technologies for Anonymity and Transparency

▶ The Policy-Aware Web

Take the class here: http://ocw.mit.edu/index.htm.

previously registered it as a fictitious or assumed name. They will still have the right to exclusive use of the name in the marketplace. Unfortunately, it's fairly common for a small business to choose a name that's similar to that of another enterprise.

There are several ways you can conduct a trademark search to avoid such problems. You can visit www.uspto.gov and do a search; pay a search firm; use a computer database; manually consult trademark registers, directories, industry journals, and other library resources; or use the phone or mail to consult state agencies. This can cost you from nothing to a few thousand dollars. Trademark searching is a competitive business, so be prepared to negotiate. Nolo Press has a self-help guide, *Trademark: Legal Care for Your Business & Product Name* that shows you how to protect your business and lists several books, software packages, and services that may help you.

Domain Name Registration

Once you have your business name, you'll need to decide on a domain name. Purchasing and registering it can be done through your ecommerce provider or you can handle it yourself through Register.com, Domain. com, DomainNames.com, Networksolutions.com, or GoDaddy.com. You can try out versions of the name you'd like on these sites and they will tell you if it's available or offer other solutions for you. For example, you may not be able to buy www.EvolveNow.com, but www.EvolveNow. biz or www.EvolveZone.com may be available. Owning the domain can cost as little as $9.99 per year. Read about incorporating your domain with a well-built website in Chapter 8.

> **tip** ⓘ
>
> Internet Corporation for Assigned Names and Numbers (icann.org) is the central registry for domain names, with more than 271 million registrations as of 2014. Find registries like GoDaddy.com, Register. com, and others by typing "domain registry" into a search engine then compare services and prices. You can register a name for up to ten years.

Insurance Is Peace of Mind

Lawsuits are in the news every day for both serious and silly offenses, which often are a result of simple mistakes and lack of education. If you deal with the public, you need insurance no matter how careful and thorough you are. Insureon's latest big data figures show most small businesses pay an average of $576 per year for either of the two most popular general liability policies:

> ▶ *$2 million aggregate.* During the lifetime of a policy, usually one year, the insurer will pay up to $2 million to cover claims.

▶ *$1 million occurrence.* The insurer will pay up to $1 million to cover any single claim. You will have to shop the market to compare what works best for you. Read more about these quotes at: www.insureon.com/insureonu/costs/general-liability.

During your research ask potential providers for cluster quotes on the other policies you may need, such as fire insurance for your office, or other natural disasters related to your geography, and health or group health for employees.

Accreditation

If offering learners academic credit or certifications is on your menu, you must be accredited in a legitimate way by a formal accreditation body. This can take several years to obtain but provides you with a necessary degree of legitimacy.

For education in an area outside of academia or a niche subject matter, each of these areas has its own governing body from which you must decide to choose accreditation. For example, if you teach food safety classes you want to get accreditation from the American National Standards Institute (ANSI) Conference for Food Protection (CFP). Law schools are accredited by the American Bar Association, medical schools by the American Medical Association or Association of Medical Colleges, and so on.

Anyone can open a business and call themselves an online university by getting a fictitious business statement and setting up a website with some course offerings, and many colleges operate for years before achieving accreditation, but students today know that a degree from an unaccredited institution is not the best value for their money since it as not as valued in the job market. To some, it has a fraudulent stigma.

These websites make it easy to earn a degree in a limited amount of time or a degree based on "life experiences."

It's important to start the process of getting accredited as soon as possible from the Council on Higher Education Accreditation (CHEA) or the U.S. Department of Education.

fun fact

What is e-discovery? Electronic discovery is the process of seeking, locating, obtaining, and securing electronic data for use as evidence in a civil or criminal legal case. Because digital data is difficult to destroy completely, it makes excellent material for supporting legal cases. Hard copy documents can be burned, but even when someone thinks they have "deleted" digital evidence the use of cyberforensics makes it possible to recover trails that lead to getting at least part of that data back.

► Beware of the Bogus Diploma Syndrome

Don't fall into any of these categories! Bogus diploma or degree mills date back to the late 1800s and still exist, selling invalidated education that doesn't hold water for students struggling to get jobs. Ten signs of a degree mill, put out by Get Educated (www.geteducated.com) are:

1. Your chosen university is not accredited.

2. Your chosen university is accredited . . . but NOT by an agency recognized by the Council on Higher Education Accreditation (CHEA, at www.chea.org) or the U.S. Department of Education (instead, by a bogus accrediting agency).

3. Admission criteria consist entirely of possession of a valid Visa or MasterCard.

4. You are offered a college degree based on a "review" of your work experience and faxed resume.

5. You are promised a diploma—an instant degree—within 30 days of application, regardless of your status upon entry.

6. You are promised a degree in exchange for a lump sum—typically $399 to $2,000 for an undergraduate degree and up to $3,000 for a graduate degree.

7. Your prospective university has multiple complaints on file.

8. Your online "admission counselor" assures you that international online universities can't be accredited in the United States by CHEA-recognized agencies.

9. The school's website either lists no faculty or lists faculty who have attended schools accredited by bogus agencies.

10. The university offers online degrees almost exclusively to U.S. citizens but is conveniently located in a foreign country, quite often a tiny nation that lacks any system of academic accreditation.

In the meantime, offer classes that clearly display fulfillment of the requirements set forth by those governing bodies.

Different forms of higher education can require different forms of accreditation and are governed by the laws of your district. Google "your state" + education commission, or higher education.

At the highest level, six regional associations handle college accreditation, which are listed on the CHEA website here: http://chea.org/Directories/regional.asp.

A Wealth of Resources

I n Chapter 2 you had the chance to take a self-inventory and refine the role you'll play in the industry. This should have left you with a clear understanding of what your eLearning identity might be. This will help you seek out the stats you need to fortify and direct your plan. Using the Bureau of Labor Statistics (www.bls.gov) might, for example, reveal how many adults in your geographic area graduated from college, how many are in a related field specific to your training topics, and how many workers there are in related corporations that may appreciate your training.

Research Today, Act Tomorrow

Collecting stats and facts on your audience is a long-range strategy to make today's patterns work for you tomorrow. Keeping track of industry news can help you anticipate how to refine your products and where to sell them—some industry tipping facts can dramatically take your business on entirely new adventures, depending on how you decide to use the information. Consider a well-thought-out market research plan an essential part of your agenda and allow daily attention to it.

Facts change rapidly in distance learning, and tracking which areas grow fastest and which tools and methods are trending over the course of years can help you calculate your best long-term direction. Elearning Industry's "2014 and 2015 Top Statistics and Facts" reports that 77 percent of U.S. companies offer online corporate training to improve the professional development of their employees, and for good reason. Productivity boosts up to 50 percent and a $30 profit return on every one dollar spent on the training keep the trend growing.

If you offer college courses, knowing that 46 percent of those students take at least one of their courses online, and by 2019 about half of all college classes are predicted to be eLearning based, can determine what you offer. According to Pew Research Center, 2015 is the year the millennials (born in the early 80s to early 2000s and also known as Generation Y) will surpass the baby boomers (born between 1946 and 1964) and the Gen X (born early '60s to late '70s) will be next in line to dominate the population, surpassing boomers in 2028. Coupled with tracking what distance learning these groups consume each year should be a supporting piece to your overall market research plan.

Other factors such as the voluntary adoption of the Common Core State Standards Initiative encourage K–12 students to prove they understand what they've learned by referring back to study materials using critical thinking, analytical, and problem-solving skills. As more states agree to measure progress by these standards, some distance educators are capitalizing on it by using the latest retention methods in their designs. How will you harness industry numbers to be the wind in your sails?

Industry Analysis

Keep investigating the numbers that count in your industry. Go to the Bureau of Labor Statistics and Census at www.bls.gov to see how many people are employed in your

▶ Book an Indulgent Research Vacation

Each year, plan a five-day hiatus that combines research, a therapeutic setting, and just you, ready to focus. If you think you can't afford to get away, think again. Dedicating a few days to uninterrupted research can bring tremendous direction and relief to your growth plan. Here's how to construct your five-day plan of attack:

▶ Choose a location that is beautiful and relaxing where there is a stimulating industry seminar or training event you can attend for the first one or two days to spark your imagination. Getting inspired before your big research endeavor will help you key into things you might not otherwise notice. See a list of events in the Appendix for ideas.

▶ Before your trip, create an outline that contains areas of importance to get the latest stats on. These can be related to areas of struggle in your business, new things you'd like to try, the most outrageous one-hit-wonders and overnight successes in your field, what your competitors are doing, and kicky new tools, software, and methods trainers are using. Certainly include updated stats for your demographic such as what their income is, where they are, how old they are, and what their priorities are.

▶ Reserve an inexpensive hotel with wifi in a picturesque setting close to your event, and plan to stay in your pajamas with good coffee and breakfast long into the morning researching the outline you've created ahead of time.

▶ Reward yourself once a day for all of your hard work with a totally indulgent break such as seeing a movie and going out to dinner, a hike at a state park, getting a massage or new hairstyle, or sitting on the beach with delicious take-out.

▶ Last, and most important, on your last day create an action plan that takes into account all of the results of your research. Organize action steps into daily, weekly, and monthly tasks.

industry each year, if their salaries rise or fall, how many dollars are being spent on the type of education you offer in your state, and if there seems to be expendable income for enrichment in the area where you live. Educational blogs, research firms, chat rooms, and government websites are good places to look for white papers and studies.

Combine Primary and Secondary Research

Primary research documents are studies and the documents written about the studies from the person or agency that conducted them. Secondary research uses a secondary course that comments about the aforementioned studies. This could be an article written by a trend watcher who conglomerates current findings from several sources to draw a conclusion, which is helpful if the writer is an industry expert and uses respected sources of primary research.

Be a Trend Watcher

One of the most important things to keep an eye on is the current trends. For example, we know that the gamification of lessons is very popular right now. Knowing that could shape the way you give information to your students—both in marketing and product development—and give you an edge. We also know that the seamless interchange of group information is being used a lot. Communities can now learn from one another with ease and collaborate on projects with sharing platforms such as Google Docs, Dropbox, and other cloud storage services. Being able to have many talents at a geographic distance from one another contributing to a single project can make a more complete product. Co-browsing and live chat software like Channel Me (www.channel.me) allows for face-to-face video meetings and the ability to look at and change the same document at the same time across the miles is invaluable. SearchTeam (www.searchteam.com) allows multiple users to search together and build a project, such as a family reunion, or hunt down valuable medical information for a loved one together. Mind42 (www.mind42.com) lets multiple users create mind maps, which are visual tracks of how a brainstorming session flows and creates new ideas. Tools like these contribute to great teamwork, and were developed by savvy trend watchers who recognized the rising popularity of collaborative work and user-generated content.

Some solid industry research sites to consult include:

▶ IBISWorld (www.ibisworld.com)

▶ Plunkett Research, Ltd. (www.plunkettresearch.com)

▶ Hoovers (www.hoovers.com)

▶ HighBeam Business (http://business.highbeam.com)

▶ Dow Jones/Factiva (http://new.dowjones.com/products/factiva)

▶ LexisNexis (www.lexisnexis.com/en-us/gateway.page)

Get to Know Your Customers

Getting to know your future customers is what good market research is all about. Conducting a thorough study of the kind of people who like products like yours doesn't just help you find them so you can send advertising their way, it helps you make a better product for them. For example, if you've created an app that helps new mothers make homemade, organic baby food in 10 minutes or less, you know that these new moms are pressed for time. Taking a deeper look at the situation by sending out a survey or holding a focus group might reveal these moms also are concerned about the higher costs of organic produce. So, why not add a tool to your product that searches the best deals and specials on organic produce by zip code? You might also realize after probing further that new moms want to understand the nutritional makeup of each food they make, so adding a nutritional tool would be smart, too. Do you see? In the beginning you were just going to offer a how-to recipe series, and now you've created a tool for almost everything they could want in one spot.

Target Market Analysis

Your marketing and business plans will be helped by good market research and show potential investors that you know what you're talking about and who needs what you've got. There are many ways to go about market research. You can spend millions of dollars targeting a general audience with consumer focus group surveys, or you can create specialized surveys for a select group of people that represents your larger audience.

Holding an event at which guests experience your product and are encouraged to give feedback is another way to do it. Repeating this presentation style market research over and over to varying groups is a good way to defray your labor costs and get the most for your money since you will be using the same presentation over and over. Offering an incentive such as a choice of select, free service coupons for guests who fill out a more detailed panel of information yields even more information because the free service they choose gives you topics for a longer conversation.

Whichever way you choose to glean valuable information from your potential client base you must create an imagined and then verified profile of who they are. Use the worksheet in Figure 5–1 on page 74 to consider your target market. After you read each question use the blanks to fill in your own ideas about your customers.

Targeting an Organization or University

If you're thinking about teaching through an organization or university, it's important to target your research toward that organization as well as at the class participant. The informational interview is a valuable tool in assessing whether your course offerings match

Target Market Research Equation Worksheet

By understanding what defines your market, such as what they like to do, what their highest priorities are, and where they work and play, you begin to also understand how to reach them.

1. What is your product? _____

2. What does it do for people? _____

3. How long does it take for them to earn the complete rewards promised in the program?

   _____

4. Why do people take your class? _____

5. What type of person takes your class? _____

6. How can you reach this kind of person? _____

7. How does that type of person best like to receive information? _____

8. How do they like to be marketed to? _____

9. What are their concerns in life? _____

10. What are five other subjects your audience is interested in? _____

    _____

11. What are their five highest priorities in life? _____

    _____

12. What do they have in common with each other? _____

    _____

13. What kind of food do they eat? _____

14. Are they interested in hobbies, and if so, what? _____

    _____

15. How do they dress? _____

16. Where do they go for fun? _____

FIGURE 5–1: **Target Market Research Equation Worksheet**

up to what a corporation or university needs. Remember that the professionals running the organization also need training to update their skill sets or certifications and that training is not just for their employees or students. Remembering this can help you take advantage of a built-in second audience when developing your products.

"Although teaching online was not initially my intention, I now feel fortunate to be part of the current flipped classroom movement designed to enhance learning by supplementing traditional teaching with online instruction. At first I was concerned about not having face-to-face time with my students. I contemplated ways to add real time sessions via Skype, for example, but in researching asynchronous strategies with the university's instructor development faculty, I was reminded that a flexible schedule is key to the majority of students who take online classes and synchronous instruction is often critical to their participation and success," Schuh says.

Focus on Focus Groups

To develop the most complete product possible that will be needed and wanted, ask several institutions pertinent to your subject matter for an informational interview that will include a sampling of administrators and students, and both employees and upper management. Tell them you'd like an hour of their time and will cater the event with pizza (or whatever) during a lunch hour so the boss won't be worried about labor costs being wasted. Ask questions like these once you get your audience:

- ▶ Is training needed at this organization?
- ▶ What kind of training would help in the areas of: communication skills, emotional intelligence, technical, self-enrichment, job specific, human resources, student orienteering, life skills, etc.?
- ▶ What does the organization see as its current biggest struggles?
- ▶ What do the employees or students see as the biggest hurdles?
- ▶ What type of delivery would work best for training sessions?
- ▶ How long and frequent would sessions be to accommodate current schedules?
- ▶ What technology, tools, and materials will participants need to take the training, and are they available?

The answers to these questions presented to several groups should shed some light on your development and marketing efforts. Even if your product idea is great and you've got your mind made up, getting information on logistics and needs can help you make it better.

If your product development is already underway, supporting your focus group or event with a sample is a good idea.

Know Your Competition

If you've decided you're going to offer an online service, including a series of online videos that trains women how to dress for success with under $500 per year (write down that business idea!), then who, you may wonder, is your competition? You have to identify your competition not just to know who is offering a similar service or product, but also to harness what they have done to your advantage. In the case of the Women's Dress for Success service, since it is a unique idea, there may not be an exact competitor match, but there may be a business that captures that part of that market's dollars. In this kind of a situation, ask yourself what your exact market spends their money on and investigate which businesses are doing well in your area. If your town has several thriving fashion resale businesses, an array of funky vintage clothing shops with quickly rotating merchandise, and large companies that employ women, you may be in the right place at the right time.

A quick search for "virtual dresser you can try on outfits online under $500 year" revealed a starting point for this exercise: Fits.me (http://fits.me)—a virtual fitting room solution.

Think about how your service might help these women who want to look unique in eclectic, but professional attire for a fraction of typical high fashion costs. It's important to market your service to people with some money to spend on learning how to save money, which may seem counterintuitive. This idea should help direct what you offer; if you were thinking of showcasing rock bottom deals on fashion and how to wear it, think again. You need to appeal to those with money to spend so you should research how much money is spent on clothing per year by your demographic and then undercut it, but not to the bottom of the barrel or you'll lose your perceived value.

Competitor Analysis

This is the place in your market research where you scrutinize what your closest competitors are doing. Some of the questions you answer will help you figure out what you should be doing to do it better than they do, or differently to gain a unique edge. Use Figure 5–2: Competitor Analysis Worksheet on page 77 to build a profile of your competitors and put together a game plan to trump them.

The Economist 2014 report, "The Digital Degree" suggests the competitor that universities must study is MOOCs. Universities have to find ways to compete with MOOCs' low startup costs and gargantuan accessibility and reach or they will sink. Harvard Business School professor Clayton Christensen considers MOOCs "a potent 'disruptive technology' that will kill off many inefficient universities" and predicts financial ruin for more than half of them within 15 years. This is what not adapting at the rate of your competition can do.

Competitor Analysis Worksheet

Who is your competition? Name a few businesses that do something close to what you do who are successful. _____

_____

_____

_____

What kind of market share do they possess? Go to Market Share Reporter (MSR) at find.galegroup. com/gdl/help/GDLeDirMSRHelp.html or IBISWorld (www.ibisworld.com) to search. _____

_____

_____

_____

How do they market their products? Is their audience the exact same as yours and if not, what are the differences? Look at their website and blog. Google "Discounts + company name" and "specials + company name". _____

_____

_____

_____

What do they lack in their services? Read reviews about them on sites like Distance Education (www.distance-education.org/Reviews/) _____

_____

_____

_____

When you read their reviews is there a common complaint? _____

_____

_____

_____

FIGURE 5–2: **Competitor Analysis Worksheet**

Hiring a Professional

You can hire a market research professional to create and host surveys for you in education industry chat rooms and bulletin boards, or do it yourself. You can also target friends and family in the initial stages of developing your questions or an interactive presentation to further hone it before giving it to the public. If you decide to hire a professional make sure she or he is well versed in distance learning. Here are some good choices for that:

fun fact

According to a prediction by TalentLMS (www.talentlms.com), a cloud-based learning management system, by 2020 the global mobile device learning market should reach $37.8 billion and by 2019 half of all college students should be enrolled in online classes.

- ► *Dr. Kay Green* (www.drkaygreen.com) is a marketing consultant and distance learning and subject matter expert specializing in advanced marketing and business courses. She's taught over 350 online courses at such prestigious universities as West Virginia, Embry Riddle, Northeastern, Arcadia, and Florida Institute of Technology.
- ► *Cayenne Consulting* (www.caycon.com) is a business plan strategist for the eLearning community that uses the three-pronged approach of competitor, target market, and industry analysis to bring a complete market research profile to your business.

► Steps to Success

The University of Professional and Continuing Education Association (www.upcea.edu) says the following action steps are paramount for unlocking key information for success in distance education:

- ► Study your customers and prospects
- ► Determine the demand for new programs
- ► Analyze online and in-the-class potential
- ► Assess and explore new market potential
- ► Measure the impact of the competition
- ► Design data-driven marketing strategies
- ► Set benchmarks with other organizations
- ► Conduct pricing and value research
- ► Plan electronic and traditional media through research

▶ *Hezel Associates* (www.hezel.com) specializes in the evaluation, planning, and research of K–12, higher education, science, technology, engineering, and math education, as well as educator professional development.

▶ *University of Professional and Continuing Education Association* (www.upcea.edu) uses electronic surveys, demographic and occupational databases, focus groups and qualitative research, competitive pricing analysis, and statistical models.

By 2020, the global mobile-learning market is on track to reach $37.8 billion, according to TalentLMS, a learning management system. (See Figure 5–3.)

FIGURE 5–3: **Athena Mediacode GmbH**
Designed for Computer and Mobile Devices (www.athenamediacode.net)

Where Is Your Audience?

The Association for Talent Development (ATD) "2014 State of the Industry" report says learning departments are responsible for providing content across a wide variety of topics and needs. About a third of their content is focused on managerial and supervisory skills, mandatory and compliance training, and profession- or industry-specific training. The remaining two-thirds cover topics such as processes and procedures, customer service, sales training, and executive development.

Every organization has unique needs and challenges that the learning function will need to address. How it does so and what it offers affects how it aligns with the benchmarking statistics presented. Just as organization size and industry influence the direct learning expenditure per employee, the types of training offered and methods of delivering training also have an impact.

Thirty-four percent of all corporate training dollars spent in 2013 falls into the top three content areas of mandatory and compliance training, managerial and supervisory training, and profession- or industry-specific training. The bottom three content categories were executive development, interpersonal skills, and basic skills, amounting to 19 percent of training dollars, according to ATD.

The Informational Interview Is Gold

Calling some of the organizations listed in the Appendix can uncover great mentor connections. Asking for an informational interview can get you five to ten minutes with top industry professionals willing to share their valuable insights. Choose entrepreneurs who do something related to what you want to do and would have a similar audience, but won't be threatening competition. Look for tech-savvy types

stat fact

The Association for Talent Development puts out an annual "State of the Industry" report, which is a great piece of research for your market research panel. The most recent year available currently is 2014, which tells us that within the corporate training arena, "manufacturing organizations, which are typically large organizations, report on average spending $535 and providing 27 hours of training per employee. Healthcare and pharmaceutical organizations spend on average $1,392 and provide 24 hours of training per employee. The combined group of finance, insurance, and real estate organizations spend on average $1,107 and provide 33 hours per employee." These kinds of facts can determine where you are more likely to mine business opportunities. If you are a member of ATD, the PDF version of the report is free. Learn more here: www.td.org.

who, even if retired, still participate actively in supporting their industries with research or informational contributions. Because virtual learning is tech dependent, it's important to learn current methods, terminology, industry standards, and the like.

Your Competitive Edge

Successful businesses have a history of being able to offer customers something either unique or that speaks to a need competitors were unable to meet. Incredible ideas don't just come from the epiphany tree or exceptionally gifted people, and usually hugely popular trends or unique businesses don't have a magical genius at the helm. They come into existence because of a series of evolutionary events. A person who is watching, calculating, recording, and analyzing needs, trends, and appetites positions themselves perfectly to strike when the time is right and is justified in doing so with all of that research.

Often an entrepreneur will have tried several other ideas or have been involved in other businesses that were conceptual stepping stones leading to the final great idea, that is, the idea no one was currently doing where a need may have not even been realized yet.

Thinkwell CEO Carl Tyson had a long history in publishing before developing the live textbook series that works so well for instructors, students, and colleges alike. His career map started by teaching at Oklahoma State University on a yearly renewable contract and not making much money. He had a wife and two kids and became attracted to a textbook sales rep job because it offered more stability, which then led over the years to becoming

▶ Wisdom from the Inventor of Pasteurization

Chemist and microbiologist, Louis Pasteur (1822–1895), changed the world by realizing the link to germs and infectious diseases, invented pasteurization and the vaccines for rabies, cholera, TB, smallpox, and anthrax. His lifelong work involved relentlessly driving himself beyond comfort and never giving up. Here are some of his insightful quotes:

- ▶ "Where observation is concerned, chance favors only the prepared mind."
- ▶ "I am on the edge of mysteries and the veil is getting thinner and thinner."
- ▶ "Let me tell you the secret that has led me to my goal. My strength lies solely in my tenacity."

Act as if you are the next Louis Pasteur of distance learning and discover and create something amazing.

a sales manager at Scott Foresman Publishing. He knew that having a Ph.D. in history put him against the wind with "about 40,000 history Ph.D.s graduating every year and only about 1,000 jobs," plus he thought the publishing industry was fun. He became the

▶ Five eLearning Business Concepts Someone Should Start!

You can rethink, piggyback, and expand on existing ideas to create new ones based on need. Here are five great concepts to get you started.

1. Training to accompany do-it-yourself cabin, modular, or tiny house kits. Customers order the homes, pull out the instructions, and then the phone calls start to the supplier. Make a brief training course that would highlight the top most common mistakes and challenges customers come across when assembling the kit.

2. Taking food production workers up to the next level. Often dishwashers wind up being chefs by paying their dues over a course of years, learning little by little, on the job. What if you offered *restaurateurs* training that would teach chefs new techniques with current food trends, teach dishwashers how to be waiters or chefs, and teach hosts how to manage the floor?

3. Food production waste and profit reduction training is always a problem in food manufacturing and restaurants. Employers often don't have the eyes and ears to monitor and correct all of the bad habits and mistakes that contribute to massive profit loss. Offering smart operational procedure training would seem worth the investment. Connecting to produce suppliers, food safety trainers, and operations managers may yield exposure to possible clients.

4. "Your First Year" relationship, partnership, or marriage training complete with the misunderstandings, conflict sources, and communication challenges most couples have and how to resolve them. The series could include funny and entertaining interviews with couples married over 50 years. Pairing up marketing with marriage service providers such as churches, Las Vegas quick wedding chapels, gown shops, specialty bakeries, and relationship therapists would be smart.

5. "Reinvent Yourself at Midlife" training to help those looking toward a second life take an inventory of the road not taken—and take it. Deep soul searching for meaningful work, activity, and world contribution plans, refreshed fashion advice, revamping one's physique, and recreating a circle of friends could be topics. Market to assisted living and memory care centers.

marketing president of McGraw Hill and, later, president of Harcourt Brace in the 1990s. That combination was quite a vantage point to study the industry from. "Then I started thinking about how the web was going to be a problem for print books. I noticed the web offered amazing potential for both effectively transferring knowledge efficiently and reaching a large audience. I thought online learning would revolutionize methodology. I was correct but of course the revolution turned into an evolution. However, I still believe digital learning offers a powerful solution to teachers, authors, learners, and businesses. Random access to highly searchable information is the first real advancement in how information is presented since consecutive pagination," Tyson says.

Don't Ignore Your Research

Experts agree that research is useless unless you act on it. Draw conclusions from the facts you collect. Create action statements that show answers to problems or voids you discover and you'll find your research takes on a new shape.

6

Finance the Dream

There is no typical way to finance an eLearning business. Some entrepreneurs secure funding, some use savings, and some create products and sell them, using the profits for growth instead of borrowing. You can harness your profits to build your business, which has its benefits. If there's a greater feeling than doing something yourself, without help, it's the feeling of not owing a dime to anyone.

Growth is great, but the negative aspect of growing as fast as your profits is that it puts a double stressor on your plans. You'll always be aware of the fact that the project you're trying to focus on today is controlling what you'll be able to fund doing tomorrow. The sanest plan, according to most of the educators in this book, is to save money or create a product that generates a steady, if not large, stream of money while you slowly grow your business. Growing your business at the rate your existing product produces profit gives you a chance to calculate your moves while gaining a deep understanding of the industry.

stat fact

According to eLearning Guild's "2015 Global eLearning Salary & Compensation Report," U.S. women report average salaries in the industry of $12,773 less than their male counterparts.

Even if you don't plan on seeking a startup loan or funding from an investor, getting ready for the process will provide several benefits to your endeavors. You'll probably need to establish lines of credit with suppliers and later on you might want to expand your business, turn it into a franchise, or even sell quickly to raise funds for a new idea. At any rate, getting your credit in order and creating a savings plan will help future investors believe in you and lend security and credibility to your business.

How Much Will It Cost?

In your first two years you'll invest in things built to last, such as product development, software, landing talent, creating company structure, obtaining offices, equipment, and all things around marketing and branding, such as website development. That means in your first year or two costs will usually be much greater than the following years because once those things have been purchased, many of them don't require as much money to maintain. Consider your first two years as investments in the future. Around year two all of the work you've spent growing your brand, landing the right customers, and showing off your products should start to help your first year expenses seem a little less intimidating as you see more and more clients purchase your coursework.

There is no set formula for determining your eLearning startup costs, but answering these questions can help you crunch the numbers required to determine your budget, starting figures, and maintenance costs.

    ► *Who will you hire to build your website and create your branding?* How much will that cost and how long will it take? Get estimates from contractors and look up salaries that represent the scope of this project.

► *How long will it take you to build the first few products that will attract a client base?* Remember that your ability to generate money is only as strong as your product is good. Don't cut corners.

► *How long will it take you to build the accompanying pieces to your product, ensuring they are technically complete and can be used in full?* Estimate your hours, weeks, or months.

► *What kind of software and equipment do you need to build those pieces?* Cost it out.

► *Will you contract your team or hire them?* If they are contractors, get rate estimates for the breadth of your complete project.

Your technical staff, IT contractors, or IT web solutions, such as your chosen CMS, comprise an ongoing investment to ensure your hard work is delivered to the client. Create a separate estimate for the maintenance programs required to deliver seamlessly. You might not know now what it will take to make that happen, but you can look at products with similar technical needs and ask those companies how IT services the product and where it comes from.

► How many team members will you hire in your first two years and what will their adjusted growth salaries be? Research and record average salaries for each job role in your geographic area.

► What kind of salary will you pay yourself?

► What are the day-to-day expenses of running an office?

► How much money will your team spend on travel and presentation expenses as you try to sell your product?

Education manager Howard B. Schechter estimates typical startup costs for a *Fortune* 1000 company to be in the $100,000 to $200,000 range and $30,000 to $50,000 for a small business or divisional learning initiative, which typically already has customer relations management (CRM) software needs accounted for.

tip

What's the difference between a course (or content) management system (CMS) and a learning management system (LMS)? An LMS is more of a training control system and is a platform or host for all kinds of eLearning courses, and provides tracking identity and completion and scoring data. It allows administrators to create reports, assignments, and reminders on the spot. A CMS is a content management application and includes editing, adding and viewing options such as security, and controls on master files and managing versions of shared documents.

Estimating how much it will take to build your first year out involves knowing how long it will take to build your product, and you might not have any idea at this point. In Chapter 3 we talked about how many hours it takes a team to create one hour of learning. The Chapman Alliance estimated an average 43 production hours are behind every hour of finished, complete learning for the student. Using that kind of formula is a good place to start.

After you build some of your first sample lessons you'll understand more specifically how many team members it will take to create a finished product. Maybe you make it all yourself, but most eLearning products at least require continuing technical help so the product is delivered smoothly.

Carl Tyson says, "There are numerous theories about how to come up with startup costs and what sort of money you need to raise. A lot depends on the source and cost of funding. If you can afford to build out your infrastructure and get a beta product going without outside funding—or with funding from friendly sources—you can enhance the valuation you get from investors. Of course, not everyone can do that. You need to estimate what the costs will be in the first six months to get going: tech, software, people, contractors, etc. Then add some percent to be safe.

▶ eLearning Salaries

eLearning Guild's "2015 Global eLearning Salary & Compensation Report" lists the top ten highest average salaries in the industry:

1. San Francisco, CA – $101,000
2. New York, NY – $97,000
3. Boston, MA – $93,000
4. Houston, TX – $93,000
5. Washington, DC – $90,000
6. Los Angeles, CA – $89,000
7. Philadelphia, PA – $85,000
8. Denver, CO – $85,000
9. Miami, FL – $84,000
10. Chicago, IL – $83,000

Globally, Australia is the place to cash in on, with the highest average salary of $105,610.

There is a critical balance between wanting to raise money to be secure—having some money in the bank to meet payroll—and raising as little money as possible early on because the valuation will be low to start. You want to sell as little of your idea as possible at low valuations."

Regardless of outside cash you may be able to raise, the SBA coaches new businesses to have one dollar in cash or business assets for every three dollars of sought loans.

If you only have $5,000 in cash, you should be looking for a business whose total startup cost is in the $15,000 to $50,000 range. The low end of that spectrum caters to those with little or no experience and the high end to an experienced business owner who can show banks a track record of repayment ability from documented cash flow management.

So what will it take to get you in business? Set up a budget and list your operating expenses for the first three months—the time it will take to create and advertise your product, and hire help. Go down the worksheet and itemize everything you will need to "open your doors" and acquire that first customer. There are so many variables that you might want to talk with retailers in your market as well as a knowledgeable SCORE counselor (www.score.org) whose background is in distance education. The tips you gather can guide you in seeing if you have enough cash on hand to do the deal, or what you'll need to get from advances on your credit cards, loans, and vendor assistance. Talk over your projections with your accountant.

Shine Up Your Credit

An absolute must is establishing two different credit profiles: personal and business. Lending institutions consider both of those credit scores when deciding if you're a reasonable risk, so if you have poor personal credit, establishing good business credit can help your average. This can give you time to work on your personal credit as well. The first thing to focus on in this multistep process is getting out of debt, if you have it.

Consumer expert Clark Howard (www.clarkhoward.com) gives these seven simple power steps to get out of debt fast:

1. Stop borrowing money and fantasizing for a lifestyle beyond your means. If you don't have money for something, don't even entertain the idea of buying it.
2. Make sure that the next time you have an emergency you've got a $1,000 emergency fund set aside for just that, rather than using a credit card to deal with the unexpected mess. That will only rack up extra expenses.
3. Stick to a realistic budget that you create by looking at what you actually spend money on.

4. Bring some extra cash into your life by, well, working a little more. Either pick up a second job or take on more freelance projects. If you're paid by the hour at your current job, ask for more hours. Clark delivered pizzas for 18 months to support his and his wife's debt-free goal.

5. Look at your budget and try to reduce certain spending areas, perhaps substituting something else that's free. For example, if you love movies and spend a ton of money on renting them, check out free DVDs galore at the library instead! You can usually keep old releases for a whole week and check out seven to ten at a time. You might have to cut your dining expenses down and make a fun food theme night at home instead.

6. List your debts from smallest to largest and pay them off that way. It will give you confidence and inspiration to cross them off the list. Another method that can save more money in the long run is to list your debts by interest rate, paying off the highest ones first. This is called laddering.

7. Any excess cash that winds up in your life, such as a car sale or tax refund, should go to paying the debts to increase the speed of them melting away.

tip

Clark Howard is crazy about saving money. It lights his fire. He's so excited about it he's compiled an extensive free and cheap list for savings on pretty much everything we humans just accept that we have to pay through the nose in life, from cell phone rates, word processing software, and cable TV, to eyeglasses, tax services, and dining deals. View: www.clarkhoward.com/the-free-and-cheap-list.

For more education on living a quality life to its fullest, pick up a copy of both of Clark's books. Clark Howard's *Living Large for the Long Haul*, which showcases 50 Americans living below their means and saving lots of money, and Clark Howard's *Living Large in Lean Times: 250+ Ways to Buy Smarter, Spend Smarter, and Save Money.*

If you have poor personal credit and can't wait for the time it takes to establish good credit, you might be able to secure a business loan with the equity in your home, but think seriously before doing this because the profit in your first two years of business can be very hard to predict.

Pay off your credit card balances and bills on time. Open a business credit card or two and use them for small things, often, and then pay the bill every month on the same day. Marco Carbajo, writer for the Small Business Administration, suggests being wary of credit before you try to get it. Just because it is offered, doesn't mean you can afford it. Credit companies don't know what your expenses are, and they don't concern themselves with your ability to pay back funds. That's up to you. Carbajo advises to consider these three points before filling out credit applications:

tip

Jim Casparie is the founder and CEO of The Venture Alliance, a national firm based in Irvine, California, that's dedicated to getting companies funded by helping you build your case and locate investor sources. Read more about how to attract venture capitalists here: www.tvausa.com.

1. Ask yourself how you intend to use the credit you receive. Will it be a day-to-day credit card used for odds and ends or a special reserve card for major expenditures? For daily use and a good habit of paying it off every month, look for a card with a low interest rate and a sizable credit limit. If you'll take a while paying for high-ticket items, then the low interest rate is very important. In both situations, look for a card with no annual fee and a long grace period.

2. Read the fine print. Don't get hooked by a low annual percentage rate (APR) only to find out after the introductory period expires you're paying a lot more than you bargained for—cancelling your card can lead to negativity on your credit report so make sure you know what you're getting into.

3. Pay ahead of the due date, and pay the entire balance monthly. Managing your business credit creates a positive credit history, so sign up for alerts on your credit report to ensure you see what others see, and only charge what you know you will be able to pay for without incurring debt.

Your Business Plan

Writing your business plan is something you'll want to do early in the game if you plan to seek funding. It shows investors the facts about your business and that you're serious and have a plan. You want to illustrate to potential investors how your business will offer a relevant, unique solution that speaks to market trends. Showing how the product generates profits by offering an affordable solution that cannot easily be copied is key. The way that new growth is expected to play out is something you should include, too. Here's a guide to structure your writing:

▶ Introduction about how your qualifications lead to running the business. Include past successes.

- ▶ Explain the product or service, how it is produced, and why it is needed.
- ▶ Explain your demographic, where you will find them, and how you will market to them. Support with research.
- ▶ Write about what your production capacity is and back it up with evidence.
- ▶ Explain why your customers will buy from you based on their current purchasing habits and your unique edge. Detail what they will pay and why.
- ▶ Break down and list how much it costs to create each product/unit or service.
- ▶ Detail how much money the company will make accounting for up and down cycles.
- ▶ Illustrate why you are asking for your startup dollar amount and what it will be used for. If it is a loan, estimate how you will pay it back and when.
- ▶ Explain how your business is viable and why it will continue to succeed, based on market research.
- ▶ Summarize the most important points of everything you have just written to a succinct list and place it at the top of your business plan. Investors will quickly glance at this to decide if they want to read further.

Tap Your Network

Networking is something that will help with all aspects of your business, especially funding, which rolls into blogging and marketing. Julie Dirksen never had to seek funding. She says she had grown a pretty substantial network when she started her business because she knew she wanted to write a book, so she leveraged the marketing with press around that book, *Design for How People Learn*, published by New Riders. When she quit her full-time job, she used her network to find consulting work. After admiring Dirksen's two-year old blog, the acquisitions editor at New Riders contacted her about writing a book. "She championed for me in the process," says Dirksen.

Carl Tyson attributes his networking base and stirring up new work to his years in the publishing industry, but says Thinkwell did seek two sources of funding in the beginning, "When I joined Thinkwell, the founders had raised a small amount from an angel investor and built the first two products, so we were then able to go to raise money from venture capital firms. That was possible in the late 1990s . . . today it is harder to find. Institutional investors will not invest today in a complete concept without products and some proof of customer/user acceptance. That is, few folks are willing today to invest in an idea. They want proof of concept. In the old parlance of venture capital, they want to make sure the dogs will eat the dog food."

Types of Funding

Look at the types of funding that you can combine to meet startup, expansion, and growth as you mature.

Personal Assets

This is a good idea if you have pure savings to use without leveraging something important, like your home, which is risky. Taking out credit card loans is also a bad idea because you don't know what kind of unforeseen circumstances will occur. But investors want to know that you are putting some solid resources on the line before they do the same, so leveraging profits from a steady producer such as getting paid for producing a few courses over time is a nice way to stockpile a budget reserve for your day-to-day business expenditures.

Loans

You need good credit and usually some saved money to get lending institutions to take a chance on you. You need to convince a lender that you have solid projections skills, are a business genius, and that your idea is accounted for in all areas of your well-written business plan. The Small Business Administration is a good source of information for business loans.

Friends and Family

Of course they want to see you succeed and to help you, but think twice about borrowing from them. It can damage relationships. But it can also work. Our advice is to go through a formal process, drafting up paperwork with the terms of the loan, and a schedule to pay back with interest, just the same way you would do with a bank. And never, ever miss a payment. Your family and friends may not be able to help you but they can help pitch your idea to people who might love the idea of acting as benefactor to a brilliant mind such as yours.

Angel Investors

These people are wealthy individuals who look for ideas to invest in and can also act as mentors through the life of your business. An experienced angel can save you time and money with their wisdom but can also cramp your style if the deal comes with wanting too much control over your plans. This is important to get clear on before accepting money from anyone.

Crowdfunding

Groups of people visit crowdfunding sites and invest in ideas they think are worth spreading. You can pitch your business idea on one of these sites and hope for interest, but you need to understand that creating a presentation to generate that interest is a project in itself. Crowdfund investors need to know their money is going toward something that they believe in, that is really going happen, rather than folding in a couple of years. Visit each of these sites with a different focus, to see how fund seekers set up their presentations:

- ► Kickstarter.com: For creative projects
- ► Indiegogo.com: Creative, personal, hobbyist
- ► Crowdfunder.com: Purely investment raising
- ► Rockethub.com: Creative with campaign guidance
- ► Somolend.com: Small business loans
- ► Appbackr.com: Mobile apps
- ► Angellist.com: Tech startups
- ► Quirky.com: Creative and community building

Venture Capital

Venture capitalists are looking for big ideas and successes to invest in. This is perhaps the most difficult funding to obtain because they have so many businesses competing for their attention and require a very high minimum investment coupled with a high exit strategy. It is difficult for most startup eLearning businesses to fit those requirements, so it is not a likely option unless your idea is extremely innovative with proven extensive growth potential. VCs can afford to be quite selective.

Partnering

While partnering with another eLearning business isn't really a funding source, it can bring a number of benefits, including some financial relief. A union of two like businesses for one cause, and streamlining a product together can bring double the rewards because of combined marketing, networking and exposure, and shared expenses. Read more about attracting attention for teamwork and investors in the Presentations section of Chapter 11.

Purchase an Existing Business

There are many benefits to purchasing an already proven business model. The concept has had time to show it has a place in the market and that the customers support it. The brand has

▶ Unsolved Mysteries

Some unforeseen expenses that can throw off your startup expenses projection are:

- ▶ Increase in taxes
- ▶ Difficulty attracting customers
- ▶ Changes in consumer habits, preferences, and demand
- ▶ New competition in your market that takes away some of your revenue
- ▶ Price increases from your suppliers
- ▶ Accidents involving you, your employees, or best customers
- ▶ Increases in insurance, utility costs, or vital supplies like heating oil or gas
- ▶ Lawsuits
- ▶ Fines

had a chance to become recognizable and established. You leapfrog ahead, skipping much of the hard work it takes to build a strong network of suppliers, customers, and advisors—that is all usually included in the purchase of an existing business. Franchises come with a high level of training and a kit that includes many of those benefits, or at least placement in an area with a pre-established record of using the service. The sale of the business is structured to allow you to reasonably pay back debt instead of creating your own structure with the unknown variables of no history in the business. This allows you to just focus on running the business instead of tying up your time with all of those startup details. Read more about buying an educational franchise at: entrepreneur.com/franchises/categories/educ.html.

Ready, Aim

Figuring out how much money you'll need is the most difficult yet vital step in the process of opening your business. It is, after all, an exercise in goal-setting. You are asked to predict what you think will happen in the first few months of something that doesn't exist yet. It's a lot easier if you are buying an existing business or a franchise because some historical or average figures can guide you.

Prepare for the unexpected when charting your startup budget. If your retail business will be your sole source of income, you will need to bankroll money to support yourself until your new venture turns a profit. Typically, the amount of money you need will equal six months' to a year's living expenses for you and your family. (See Figure 6–1 on page 96.)

Startup Expenses Worksheet

Accountant setup fees	$
Advertising	$
Cash register	$
Computer system	$
Fixtures	$
Grand opening	$
Insurance	$
Inventory setup and pricing	$
Legal fees	$
Licenses and permits	$
Miscellaneous expenses	$
Office equipment	$
Opening inventory	$
Payroll account	$
Remodeling	$
Rent/security deposit	$
Retail seller's permit deposit	$
Shop equipment and tools	$
Shop supplies	$
Signs	$
Supplies (office, cleaning)	$
Utility deposits	$
Subtotal	$
Miscellaneous expenses (10 percent of subtotal)	$
Total Startup Expenses	$

FIGURE 6–1: **Startup Expenses Worksheet**

Diane Elkins developed her company little by little as she worked a 30-hour per week corporate account that kept her mortgage paid. This left her a little time to do all the things over the course of a year that needed to be done to start her business.

Homebased Businesses Aren't Free

Although a homebased business won't have all the expenses of a leased-space business, it is rare for any type of retailer not to have startup expenses. You will need supplies and business equipment. Laws and ordinances governing homebased businesses vary widely from community to community. Know what is required before you start yours.

A homebased business may need a license to operate, a seller's permit, and a federal ID number, depending on your industry and local requirements. You should also check fire

► Tips for Successfully Working from Home

Heather Wilson, author of the *E-Learning Uncovered* series (http://elearninguncovered.com) suggests five tips to keep you sane if you work from home:

1. *Get dressed every day.* It's good for your self-esteem, you never know when you'll have an impromptu Skype call or lunch date, and it'll keep you happy with yourself when you have to look in the mirror.

2. *Get some exercise every day.* Studies show brains on exercise function better. It's hard science, so just do it! Fifteen minutes of sit-ups, climbing stairs, or burpees (a quick, high-exertion exercise) can increase blood flow to your brain and help you mine new ideas hidden way down deep. Learn how to do a burpee here: http://en.wikipedia.org/wiki/Burpee_(exercise). One benefit of working at your home is that you can have your dog at work—take the dog for a walk for a refreshing break!

3. *Get away from work at lunch.* Just getting away for half an hour will give you fresh eyes and an invigorated second wind. A walk in the park or lunch somewhere outside resets your nerves and soothes the soul.

4. *Get a schedule and stick to it.* Time can drift into a vacuum at home with all kinds of distractions. It's important to clearly define when you start, when you'll break, and when work is absolutely over.

5. *Get an "in the office" friend.* Connect with someone also working from home or a professional you respect by phone for quick chats or lunch to keep you stimulated, well advised, and social.

department permits if you use flammable materials; air and water pollution control permits if you plan to burn any material or discharge any waste into the waterways; liquor, wine, and beer licenses if you sell liquor, even through the mail; and health department permits if your business involves food or food preparation.

You may be sufficiently covered under your existing homeowner's or renter's policy, or you may need additional insurance coverage. Check with your insurance agent. And to find out what tax benefits you may qualify for with your homebased business, seek the guidance of an accountant who is familiar with homebased deductions. He or she can calculate your cash needs with and without the tax deductions, in case tax laws change and you receive no benefits beyond savings on rent and utilities.

tip

There are five things an entrepreneur should be prepared to show a loan officer: a business plan that shows how you will use the financing to operate the business, proof that you pay your obligations when due, that you have enough equity money, that your team has enough experience to implement the plan, and that your sales prospects are strong enough to repay the loan.

Bank Locally

Regardless of your location, as a businessperson, you'll need to set up your accounts. You want a bank that wants your business. Look for a full-service financial institution that caters to small businesses in general and retailers specifically. Your goal is to find one that has the products, services, and fees that fit your needs.

The basic items you will want to compare among financial institutions are:

▶ Business checking account
▶ Business interest checking account
▶ Business savings account
▶ Cash management services
▶ Merchants' deposit
▶ Payroll service
▶ Online banking services
▶ Lines of credit (seasonal and revolving)
▶ Small-business loans (short-term, long-term, collateral, equipment, accounts receivable financing, factoring accounts receivable, cosigner)
▶ SBA-approved status

▶ Wire transfers
▶ Deposit box rental
▶ Foreign currency exchange

Even if you're planning on using savings to start your business instead of taking out a loan or getting outside investors, it's always a good idea to be on a first-name basis with your bank for future expansion loans. Establish relationships with bankers at networking functions such as meetups, chambers of commerce, industry events such as those held by ATD and eLearning Guild, and Networking International.

> **tip** ⓘ
>
> Weigh the fees charged and services offered by different banks against their proximity to your business, hours of operation, cooperativeness of personnel, and the bank's reputation for working with retailers.

Put the bank manager and head of the loan committee on your mailing list; say hello or wave when you're in the bank, and make a point to share some exciting news with them about sales, new personnel, or your community involvement. By being someone they know and respect who doesn't want anything from them, when you do approach them to get some new equipment, remodel your store, or even to provide a reference, they will know who you are.

Location, Location, Location

Location is always significant to the success of a business, even distance learning. While obviously your customers are not coming to your location, you need to be in an area where you can be successful as a business person and where you can attract high-level employees (who don't all, of course, need to be local to your business' location but some will need to be).

The professionals interviewed for this book attribute personal networking to the success in almost every area of their business. They also told us how important it is to be in a city where exciting things are happening in an exciting, technologically oriented, modern industry. Watching average salaries paid to techies is a big tip off to the areas that meet this criteria. Currently the top ten cities on that list are:

1. Silicon Valley, CA
2. Baltimore, MD
3. San Diego, CA
4. Boston, MA
5. Seattle, WA
6. Houston, TX
7. Los Angeles, CA
8. Denver, CO
9. Sacramento, CA
10. Austin, TX

Combine that list with Getting Smart's (www.gettingsmart.com) "10 Smartest Cities" list and you'll see a lot of overlap. This one is based on criteria such as innovation mindset, sustained leadership, talent development, collective impact, new tools and schools, and advocacy and policy:

1. New York, NY
2. Silicon Valley, CA
3. Washington, DC
4. Boston, MA
5. San Francisco, CA
6. Chicago, IL
7. New Orleans, LA
8. Denver, CO
9. Oakland, CA
10. Houston, TX

Other factors such as initiatives like the Next Generation Learning Challenges should be part of your consideration about where to establish roots as these are signs of growth and promise. This new effort pairs with established Education Cities (cities committed to improving public school education, see http://education-cities.org) to provide support for creating upgraded education to include expert coaching, self-paced learning.

- ▶ Battelle Education (Central Ohio)
- ▶ Center for Collaborative Education (Boston)
- ▶ Choose to Succeed (San Antonio)
- ▶ Excellent Schools Detroit
- ▶ The Marshall L. and Perrine D. McCune Charitable Foundation (Santa Fe, NM)
- ▶ The Mind Trust (Indianapolis)
- ▶ New Schools for Baton Rouge
- ▶ Project Renaissance (Nashville)
- ▶ Rhode Island Mayoral Academies
- ▶ Schools That Can Milwaukee

Keep track of the trends that make sense for your business. Look for news about where large investments are going, both public and private. Even though it can take years for those investments to change the landscape of education in that area, it's wise to keep track and base your decisions on areas where you see patterns of growth.

Setting up an office for an eLearning business often is done by professionals who had previously been working from home. Young startup companies can be unaware of what the future holds and want to keep expenses down, but find that commercial landlords want a hefty commitment—usually a five- to seven-year lease agreement. Signing on for an extended time agreement in an office that doesn't account for future wild cards can be scary. You may increase your staff five-fold in the next few years and if your space doesn't fit that growth it could hurt unless you plan for that growth in staff to be mostly remote workers.

Look for space that either fits your long-term growth plan or has a shorter lease. The disadvantage to that, though, is that your rent can and will most likely be raised at each lease renewal period without the safety of a long-term lease. Subleases are an option and can be found by searching similar businesses and teaming up with them, which is smart because the space is already designed for similar use.

Whether you are going to remodel or build from the ground up, consider all the things that will be happening in your building before choosing. Make a list of all the activities and their privacy, equipment, noise level, electricity, and atmospheric requirements. Here are some of the things that might go on at a typical eLearning office:

- ▶ *Presentations.* Show clients new product and let them engage in it in an environment that simulates the typical student environment. Demonstrations in a formal presentation style and individual-use stations should be accounted for as well as all of the AV equipment and furniture needs.

▶ *Individual spaces* with enough privacy and quiet for employees, but room and space for creative collaboration.

▶ *Workspace trends* that are designed to increase productivity include comfortable, relaxing, but social nooks near common areas. This increases the possibilities of "chance encounters" with other employees and opportunity for creativity. Creating a space where workers can adjust tables and chairs and daily restructure their space needs according to project is important. Adjustable desks and chairs that people can sit on or stand at reduce stress on the body and mind. This will factor into your choice of furniture as well as office layout. Don't skimp on comfort or the psychological results will negatively affect your bottom line.

▶ *Reception and greeting.* The latest trends in office design encourage the whole staff to greet customers by making the reception area open and not separate from the offices so that guests can feel the energy of the hive and workers can welcome them in.

aha!

Creating relaxation stations for your employees need not be expensive and can increase productivity.

Consider making cubbies with these elements for breaks and renewed energy:

▶ *A yoga station.* With mats, yogi music, and meditative lights
▶ *Friday lunch hour chair massage.* Hiring a chair massuesse isn't expensive
▶ *Ping pong table.* Ping pong is all the rage, helps let off steam, and certainly produces laughter, the great diffuser
▶ *Pets allowed.* Though some people are allergic to pets, sectioning off part of the building for them is smart as it can create a bonding between employees, reduce stress, and allow them to work longer hours when they don't have to get home to let the dog out.
▶ *Workout rooms and treadmill desks.* Sitting is the new death stamp. It's all over the news with recommendations to get up every hour for at least ten minutes. Treadmill desks can work if employees can share a few to keep costs down. Standing chairs can be used for part of the day, too. Having your office near a place to take short walks is helpful.
▶ *Healthy snacks.* Either make healthy vending available or create an opportunity in the break room for employees to easily make healthy snacks like smoothies, raw veggies and salads, or heat up or cook a community pot of stew.
▶ *An altar of spirituality.* One that recognizes all religions and alienates none. This can be a quiet, sunny meditation and prayer room with overstuffed chairs, soft music, candles, and spiritual art made by employees.

▶ *Library.* Not just a boring industry news library, but one that relates many other areas of life to eLearning with works of literature and photo albums.

Parking

If your office is divine but the parking creates a nightmare for guests and employees, this can be a problem. Workers can be distracted by having to move their cars every few hours or getting tickets, which will affect productivity. Guests can arrive frazzled, which will change their experience with your product or service. If you have a city location and metered or pay lot parking is your only option, then have quarters ready for people that need them and offer parking validation discounts.

B2B Partnering

Business to business relationships can make a wonderful community atmosphere. Consider doing a trade with the coffee shop or juice bar down the street in exchange for discounts for employees. You can offer trading businesses free demos of your products for their parties, or use of your yoga room for their employees.

Equipment

You'll need the usual array of office equipment and will want to utilize low cost and creative options for this, depending on the look and feel you are going for. Some options for this are:

▶ Hiring a staging professional who creates displays entirely with used furniture from consignment shops, Craigslist, and estate sales. These people often have access to discounted new furniture as well and can help you come up with a unique look.

▶ Hire an interior design student to create your space under budget. Look at portfolios and past design projects, and ask for their intended plan of operation.

Software and Hardware

There are so many software and hardware choices for eLearning providers that it's hard to predict what you'll need exactly until you finish writing your business plan and create some of your first courseware pieces. But here are some general categories by function that comprise a lot of what distance educators use.

► Tally Up Your Office Needs

Your needs will vary depending on your output, product, number of employees, and type of eLearning business. Here is a list with some of the typical things you might need related to opening up an office.

- ► Phone lines
- ► Rent and utilities
- ► Internet
- ► Basic office equipment and furniture
- ► Office supplies
- ► Computers
- ► Back-up drives or cloud space
- ► Laser printer
- ► Software
- ► Website, web design, and hosting
- ► Insurance
- ► Legal and accounting services
- ► Licenses and permits
- ► Subscriptions to trade journals
- ► Association membership dues
- ► Advertising and marketing
- ► Miscellaneous supplies

Computers

No old technology! Be sure you have the computer power you need with the highest memory and largest monitor (17 to 23 inches is almost standard these days) you can afford. These are the things that make you efficient and effective and should not be considered a poor use of money.

Laptops are important to be able to move around and give demos at changing locations. Laptops that serve as desktop computers with comfort features such as a detachable full keyboard, wireless mouse, and separate monitor that can all be detached for portable use are a great way to combine all the features needed to provide highly productive electronics for the office.

Mobile devices such as smartphones, tablets, and MP3 players will let you view and test software you've built expressly for these devices in real time, as well as keep up on your social media postings. If your car does not have built-in Bluetooth, be sure to get a Bluetooth device to use for phone calls while traveling. Most states are moving to laws that do not allow use of any handheld devices.

A high-quality microphone, speakers, and a headset will allow you to hold video chats and record audio files for sharing.

Printer/scanners get used daily in a variety of ways by most offices. It's good to have access to an all-purpose one. Most contemporary printers have built-in scanners and copiers and are very zippy in their pages-per-minute print speed—just keep in mind that replacing the ink cartridges is where the real costs add up.

Ensure you have back-up drives or storage such as:

▶ Cloud storage solutions like Google Drive (www.Google.com/Drive), Dropbox (www.dropbox.com), or Apple iCloud (www.Apple.com/icloud)

▶ External hard drives such as the Western Digital Raid 1 8TB My Book Thunderbolt, and AirPort Time Capsule.

▶ Off-site paper storage. Keep paper copies of all important data and store it in a warehouse or building off-site.

Software can usually be purchased by yearly subscription or flat fee, sometimes with options that let you store some of your data in the cloud. When it's time for an upgrade, you'll be notified and either asked to pay an upgrade fee if you've only paid for a year. Regular updates are usually free once you've purchased the software outright. Most software comes with free tutorials that can be accessed from its website.

Because of the massive use of mobile devices to access eLearning, a shift is taking place in the software and services area that incorporates HTML5, a technology mark-up language for the internet and how it presents content. HTML5 allows users to take their lessons with them, accessing them on any device, and uses less CPU space and battery power to display interactive eLearning courses. What this means for you as you select software is that you have a choice to make. Do you want to go with the future and allow users to access your lessons everywhere or use older software and make the upgrades later? These authoring packages come with combinations of features to create engaging eLearning courses such as dynamic graphics, audio, cloud storage, marketing, sales processing/ecommerce, content management, mobile-design specific tools, presentation tools, video lecture, PowerPoint add-in converter, games and virtual worlds. Here is list of popular HTML5 authoring tools:

▶ Adapt Learning (www.community.adaptlearning.org)

▶ H5P (www.h5p.org)

▶ Lectora Inspire (www.lectora.com)

▶ Brainshark (www.brainshark.com)

▶ Rapid Intake (www.litmosauthor.com)

▶ Ready Go (www.readygo.com)

▶ SHIFT (www.shiftelearning.com)

▶ Zenler Studio (www.zenler.com)

Choosing training platform software doesn't need to be hard. Make a list of what you need it to do for you and your clients and then start looking for a match. DigitalChalk demonstrates some of the basic components of a good platform package:

▶ *Chalkboard.* Helps you create mixed media presentations with video, audio, slides, HTML, and other images.

▶ *Web archive.* Allows you to embed course content from various media sources.

▶ *Testing.* Helps you create tests with multiple choice and true/false answer possibilities.

▶ *File linking.* Refers learners to stored documents for viewing, such as spreadsheets and PDFs, with a button or link.

▶ *SCORM.* Assists in transferring content from authoring tools and learning management systems.

▶ *PowerPoint converter.* Helps turn your PowerPoint presentations into lessons.

▶ *Assignment collection.* Lets you assign and collect student tasks, tests, and workbook assignments.

▶ *Certificate awarding.* Gives the ability to plant certificate earning anywhere within your curriculum and award them to learners.

> **tip** ⓘ
>
> The ATD Buyer's Guide (http://webcasts.td.org/sites) is a comprehensive directory of learning and development providers and a good place to look for technical solutions to your business's unique challenges. Attending trade conferences is another way to learn about the latest software and hardware solutions. Exhibitors are set up to let you test everything out and they have a lot of time to conceptually customize the way you might use their products, giving you more ideas for development. The eLearning Guild conferences and expos are once such place to do that: www.elearningguild.com/content.cfm?selection=doc.24.

Other things you might need depending on your goals are:

▶ Audio recording: Garageband, Audacity

▶ Movie editing: iMovie, Windows Movie Maker

▶ Math/engineering: Wolfram

▶ Graphics editing: CorelDRAW, Picasa, Adobe Illustrator or InDesign

▶ Photo editing and organization: Adobe Photoshop

▶ Word processing and spreadsheets: Microsoft Office Professional bundle includes Word, Excel, and PowerPoint

▶ Presentation, promotion, and communication: Microsoft PowerPoint and Publisher. Note that while PowerPoint presentations can be converted to eLearning courses easily, caution must be exercised to use creativity and common sense with parsing out sections to different media

▶ Accounting, sales, paying bills, scheduling, tracking invoices, and daily transactions: QuickBooks Pro, Sage 50 Accounting, and Acclivity (www.acclivitysoftware.com/) Accounting (formerly, M.Y.O.B., Mind Your Own Business)

Your eLearning Website

The goals of an eLearning website are to connect the learners and trainers with an elegant design that intuitively guides complex interactions without glitches, sells the product, and conveys what the company stands for. Of course, as an online-based business, the pressure is slightly higher for your website to reflect the high quality of your courses' online experience. While you don't need to spend your entire startup budget on website design and creation, do not shortchange the site either.

Your website should be able to display all your creativity and allow for easy technical solutions that don't rely on someone who makes you wait or stays on the phone for hours while you lose money because of downtime. People should understand who you are easily and fairly quickly after landing on your site. Web design is an art that takes into account how many seconds a person is willing to stay on a page, anticipates the motion of their vision, and focuses on filling needs and capturing information quickly.

There are some great web design companies that offer sharp solutions developed expressly for eLearning products. Choosing the right web design provider involves making an assessment of your needs and going over each of the provider choices to see which offers the closest fit. Here are some of the things a combination LMS/web host/design service can offer to fill your needs:

- ► Course creation
- ► Student registration
- ► Sales
- ► Certification management
- ► Live video conferencing
- ► Tests, quizzes, and assessment management
- ► Student portals/forums

The core of your website will be determined by the LMS you choose. LMS types are divided into three categories: open source, SaaS (Software as a Service)/cloud, and proprietary learning.

With proprietary learning the upfront costs are high, but you own the design through purchased licensing. This is what most large organizations and universities use.

Open source has fees associated with it, usually based on your enrollment or a monthly charge. While there are no fees to license it, you have to pay for hosting and the optimization of the software for your purposes and those costs can add up. Open source allows for growth and change because it is easily altered; for a young, growing company, this is a good thing.

The benefits of using an SaaS/cloud LMS are that upgrades are included, storage costs are low and able to accommodate vast amounts of data, there is no

save

A free guide to help you calculate your return on investment with all things considered within these choices is available here as a free download: www.webanywhere.us/ our-blog/open-source-vs-proprietary-lms.

maintenance, it is very secure, and once your options are chosen, deployment is very fast.

One option that a lot of people first starting out use is an open source LMS platform, which you can modify for your own purpose, and then publish and reoffer it as your own to the community. Moodle (www.moodle.com) is one choice of an open source LMS. Moodle is pretty high-end with almost any feature you could ever need in an eLearning website, as it was originally designed for universities. It also has the capability of using plug-ins for new things you'd like to try that aren't part of Moodle's package. Moodle isn't the easiest software to learn and doesn't have ecommerce tools built in, but it plays well with WooCommerce (http://woocommerce.com), an ecommerce plug-in, is very secure, and has lots of collaboration tools for you and your students.

Or you can build your website on WordPress (www.wordpress.com) using any of its LMS themes, which in essence are one-stop-shop solutions to anything you could need. WordPress's theme WPLMS, also partners with BuddyPress (www.buddypress.org) so that you can create your own social media platform for students and teachers to build a community with. It uses WooCommerce as a plug-in ecommerce solution.

Another option is to build your site on WordPress and use an LMS plug-in, such as LearnDash (www.learndash.com), which is often paired with WordPress for eLearning solutions. This allows you greater flexibility in controlling how your site looks, rather than being restricted by the LMS theme in the previous option. A fun and useful event management plug-in called EventEspresso can be used to coordinate lectures and other in-person elements of your course with the virtual. Gravity Forms is another plug-in that can be used with this plan to create forms to capture information. There are plug-ins available for many tasks that allow a more creative product.

Most people without tech backgrounds find it easiest to use a plan like WordPress either way rather than Moodle to set up their website if they're doing it themselves. If hiring a team including IT staff is on the menu, then it's not an issue; they can handle not just figuring that out but also what system will work best for your product.

Services like Capterra (www.capterra.com) can help connect you with the right provider to match your needs after filling out a short set of questions.

Here are examples of LMS options.

Open source learning management systems:

▶ Canvas by Instructure (www.instructure.com/)
▶ eFront (www.efrontlearning.net/)
▶ Fedena (www.fedena.com)
▶ Moodle (https://moodle.org)

▶ Sakai (https://sakaiproject.org)

SaaS/cloud learning management systems:

▶ DoceboLMS (www.docebo.com)
▶ EduWave (www.itgamerica.com/eduwave-k-12)
▶ Expertus One (www.expertus.com/expertus-one/)
▶ Litmos (www.litmos.com)
▶ TalentLMS (www.talentlms.com)

Proprietary learning management systems:

▶ Blackboard Learning System (www.blackboard.com)
▶ Desire2Learn (https://opencourses.desire2learn.com/cat/)
▶ eCollege (www.ecollege.com/index.php)
▶ Engrade (www.engrade.com)
▶ GlobalScholar (http://globalscholar.us)
▶ JoomlaLMS (www.joomlalms.com)

Joomla! is a web design service that can incorporate and manage many of the elements you'll need to create, interact with, and keep everything running smoothly. Joomla! and other proprietary management systems offer a combination of services like these:

▶ Gets your courses online and running
▶ Allows you to customize your content easily
▶ Uses data analytics to understand your customers better
▶ Tests visual design and functionality
▶ Tests template function
▶ Social media integration
▶ eCommerce capability
▶ Mobile device design
▶ Website configuration and installation
▶ Add-on components like calendar and photo gallery
▶ Sells your courses

aha!

Hire a web designer like Dan Paul and it will take a lot of the guesswork out of choosing the many elements that need to go into your website. Dan specializes in eLearning web design and has a portfolio that spans medical device training modules, eardrum surgery simulations, and military first responder training as well as corporate training for companies such as Bank of America. View Paul's beautiful work here: www.dan-paul.com.

Website Components

Write down a detailed list of several goals different customers may have when landing on your site and how they will travel through the channels to achieve their goal. Make sure it's easy and enjoyable. Ask friends and family to test navigating your site before committing to a design.

The same priorities other businesses use in conveying mission, introducing staff, and providing easy solutions for shoppers are important for an eLearning site. A wealth of resources, including demonstrations of your product should also be provided as well as a content rich blog and links to social media. Let's look at the usual and necessary website components for building your relationship with potential eLearning customers.

Welcome/Home

The look of this page should convey everything about your mission, product, and branding with images, layout, and design. Buttons or icons to easily accessed product demos should be obvious on the homepage. A current website trend is featuring a huge, striking image on the welcome page, rather than many. A rule for the homepage is that no matter where you are within the site you should be able to get back to the homepage easily—that is the place where you can access everything else through a menu of single clicks.

About Us

There are advantages to putting your mission statement on your website homepage so that readers have a strong impression of what you do before they get to the About Us section. There they should read how each member of your team fits in with the mission. You can also put your mission on its own page and reiterate it on your team page, but if you've developed a vision statement, that generally works well on the About Us page.

The About Us section on your website should show the world your credentials, goals, perhaps how you started your company, and a little of your personality. Because you are a virtual firm, each page on your site needs to make just the right impression, and lead logically to the next page.

tip

Blogging is important to your business. Google favors you based on how many relevant blog posts you create with quality content for users looking for your kind of topics. Do you want to be found and promoted to higher page rankings? A blog as part of your website will take the whole site to stardom if you're a good enough writer and give your market what it craves reading about.

You and your team members should be proud of the accomplishments that have led you to provide your high-quality service and that should show in the content on this page. Listing some of your high-profile clients (once you get them and with their permission), significant projects, and B2B relationships here is appropriate if done in a biography style. A little humor or information about who you are as a person outside of work is sometimes appropriate, depending on what kind of clientele you're trying to reach. You could add something that talks about a personal interest you have and tie it into something about your product, such as, "In his spare time, Jim loves surfing California's wild coast while dreaming up new courseware."

A classy, professional photo of each team member lends some solidity that yours is a real service and not just a business that hopes to get some action but hasn't the real talent behind it. Anything you can do to set yourself apart from the degree mills and scammers without any substance behind their claims is good. Cross-linking to business sites you work with gives additional credibility.

Company Philosophy and Mission

This is about who you are at your core. It is where your ethics intersect the products you sell and the way you treat the world, including customers and employees. Linking to your achievements in the education field, or any initiatives you support with your curriculum is appropriate here. Make sure this page conveys the best of what you do in credentials, accreditation, and any other stamps of approval from governing bodies.

Product Pages and Shipping/Checkout

Your ecommerce solutions should be smooth and obvious. If you'll be charging a monthly fee at three levels for different subscription types for learning, then make that clear and all in one place. Visitors to your website should be able to get more information about a product, or a 1-800 help line here, too.

Landing Pages

Landing pages are where you are routed to when you click on a product for details and options. They are for all education about products for your customers.

Choose a Website Builder or Hire a Pro

You can design your own website with access to good photo editing software like Photoshop and a low-cost website building service such as Wix.com, GoDaddy.com,

BuildYourSite.com, Fatcow.com, and Web.com. They offer step-by-step guides to coach you through the process. You can also hand over all of the responsibility to a professional website developer or choose a lower-cost option, such as a design student or new business looking for pieces to add to its portfolio. You may also have to hire a writer if your chosen design professional doesn't excel in that area. Make sure to read reviews, and check references for anyone you are considering hiring, rather than just looking at the fancy work they've designed. Customer service is key and will mean a lot in the future when you need quick changes made to your online presence. Look on Yelp.com for businesses offering discounts, search Craiglist.org for contractors, and ask friends and relatives for connections to low-cost website designers.

One-Stop-Shop Solutions

Many of your needs can be covered by choosing service providers that perform several functions, such as:

▶ *Yahoo! Merchant Solutions* (http://smallbusiness.Yahoo.com/ecommerce), a hosting site that helps you design an online store and set up a merchant account to accept and process credit card orders.

▶ *Volusion* (www.volusion.com), *Affinity Internet* (www.affinity.com), and *1&1* (www.1and1.com) are hosting companies with shopping cart, merchandising, and shipping technologies, and marketing assistance.

▶ *osCommerce* (www.osCommerce.com) allows store owners to set-up and run their online stores for free, with ecommerce solutions, of course.

We're Hiring

Create an optional section on your website that coordinates your mission statement with your desire to find employees cohesive with it. Don't just list job openings and define roles— help readers understand the main goals of your company and how they'd support them. Yanay Zaguri's free ebook *5 Steps to a Successful Onboarding Process* (www.kryonsystems.com) will help the way you write and display employment on your website.

Get Your Web House Ready for Guests

Before you set up any kind of official presence, you should be ready for guests. Think of it like having surprise visitors to your home. If the doorbell rings, what would you like guests to see when they visit? How would you like to come across to them? Would you like to answer the door in your bathrobe with moisturizer smeared all over your face and the remnants of a cookie spilled down the front of your robe? We didn't think so.

The way to ensure you take advantage of those first few guests is to think of their visits as precious. Know they may never come back again if everything isn't impressive, sharp, innovative, unique, and expressing excellent quality and customer service. The first category to focus on to display on your site is the actual work you will be doing for others, in the form of a demo. It will take some time to translate your wonderful ideas to short demos that spark the viewer's interest, taking care to not give away content that will make money for you in the full versions of the lessons.

There are several sites that coach you through building your first lessons, and some are free. Most of these sites have very valuable resources that can be mined for trends, industry connections, and webinars.

▶ *ELearningtemplates.com.* Lesson templates with graphics and stock libraries, $499 per designer per year.

▶ *Academyofmine.com.* All-in-one platform to create, sell, and market courses, $199 to $449 per month.

▶ *DigitalChalk.com.* Course production services to create and deliver courses, $206 and up.

What Will Your Site Do?

The most important facets of your courses will either shine or be lost according to how you put your site together, deliver the information to the learner, and provide answers to every "why?" that comes up. The elements that create a complete, highly functioning distance learning website vary by purpose and goals, but there are a few general areas that most professionals have to consider and are essential to ensuring the learner's ultimate experience.

My website helps me by:

▶ Utilizing captured data for future connections and selling opportunities

▶ Helping me stay organized and abreast of sales/ecommerce changes

▶ Letting me see who has liked me or my blog on social media channels

▶ Helping me see which areas of navigation are and are not working through site analytics

▶ Creating a professional presence and acting as a virtual business card

Big Data

Capitalizing on big data is key to understanding patterns indicating where your customers come from, what they look for on your website, what they buy, and what they click on but don't buy. When you attach data services to your website, you access information that is like a glimpse inside the collective customer mind, enabling you to customize a better business for that mind and capture more sales. Sales processing services such as ShopKeep (www.shopkeep.com) and LightSpeed (www.lightspeedpos.com) also offer data collection to businesses, but it's up to you to review and use the data to your advantage and change your behavior accordingly.

Offer Video

In a *Business News Daily* (www.businessnewsdaily.com) interview, Tom Malesic, president and CEO of web design firm EZSolution, said using videos can be like getting free commercial time and, "Consumers are more likely to purchase after seeing a video than if there was no video at all." Linking your website to your own YouTube channel is a great way to extend the product education dialogue your website begins with customers. Each thumbnail of a product can show a larger image when clicked on and, as utilized on Zappos.com, a short video could be accessed to showcase the product in context. You can also embed videos on your site, but using YouTube is often easier when it comes time to make changes and update videos and keyword tags that search engines use to find them. Because YouTube is a Google

▶ Your Age-Smart Jobs Section

Human resource consultants Ellie Klevins and Nancy Mason help employers relate to and attract the right employees in all age groups. Using the communication style that each particular group is most adept at is key to maximizing communication during the hire and employment process, and studying the strengths and weaknesses of each of these groups will help you write appropriate ads for the "We're Hiring" section of your website. Each of these groups is most fluent in a different style:

- ▶ Seniors born 1920–1945 prefer handwritten notes and letters.
- ▶ Baby Boomers born 1946–1965 do best with phone calls.
- ▶ Gen Xers born 1966–1979 are most engaged in email.
- ▶ Gen Yers born 1980–2000 text just about everything.

product, when Google+ users comment on your video, it automatically posts on Google+, potentially expanding your viewing audience.

warning

Keep up on your training. It's easy to feel overwhelmed by all of the training you need to give others and skimp on your own. If you do this, you may be missing the boat on using new technologies.

Ongoing Training Is Imperative

In his report, "Distance Learning: Promises, Problems, and Possibilities," Doug Valentine of the University of Oklahoma cautions against misuse of technology, a common blunder among trainers.

"Besides the cost of the technology, there is the possibility of not utilizing all its potential. Some of these problems arise from a lack of training, some from the instructor's attitudes about using the technology, and still others by hardware problems. It seems to be self-evident that instructors need to be trained to use distance learning technology, but too often they are not. Once again, it appears that administration may feel that the technology itself will improve the course. Advancement in technology does not lead to effective distance education." Valentine adds that the skills and knowledge of the instructors themselves are what make the best distance learning, along with a complete understanding of how to use the technology and shift their knowledge to it.

Here are some places to ensure you keep on top of your own training:

▶ The Center for Instructional Development and Distance Education (www.cidde. pitt.edu)

▶ Smart Technologies Live Online Training and Distance Education (www.smart tech.com)

Social Media Practices

Students who learn online already face a bit of an isolation factor. It's important to build an online and real-time community that serves to make them feel part of a caring group with shared values. Phone calls, video chats, participating in forums, and creating special, personalized contributions to social media can build strong relationships with your students and increase their chances for success in your classroom and serve as a mentorship for years to come.

Even though business owners tend to think of social media's role as something that serves their business, for distance educators it's more than that. Because more of the truly important functions that are the life of the business occur online, taking relationships seriously within the social media realm should be a priority. You can influence your students' grades, participation, hopefulness about school, and outlook on life by your contributions to social media, which is just another way to gift your audience.

Steven Starks, senior academic counselor at the University of Phoenix lists eight engagement tips in his interview, "Exploring Retention Strategies for Distance Learners," with The Evolllution (www.evolllution.com) to help build relationships between student and teacher:

1. *Student success webinars.* Engage students by hosting live webinars! This can be a meet-and-greet opportunity in which students meet their support team (academic advisors, faculty, etc.) or learn tips and strategies for success. Webinars can occur prior to the beginning of the program or throughout the entire program in order to enhance student preparedness by offering relevant and useful information about campus resources, policies, or procedures.

2. *Supportive calls and emails.* Advisors can contact students for telephonic advising sessions, use email templates with succinct messages that offer useful information, or send motivational messages.

3. *Social media.* Meet students where they are by creating a Facebook page, Twitter account, or YouTube channel to broadcast messages about campus news and events, remind students of important deadlines, or inform students of certain opportunities. Institutions could also create a blog that addresses strategies for success.

4. *Orientation.* Design an orientation for students that provide them with a list of resources and contacts prior to their start date. Address expectations and orient students to the online environment and the resources available to them

5. *Advisor chat.* Designate specific times when students can chat with their advisor using an instant messaging/chat client for basic questions and answers.

6. *Resource portal.* Develop a portal that enables students to get the latest information or access to resources, a central location that is easy to find and use.

7. *Establish learning communities.* Learning communities can be integrated into an existing LMS or academic/social engagement network or created through the use of free resources such as EdModo.

8. *Mine data.* Measure as much as you can and use the data to make informed decisions and track course completion rates and satisfaction measures.

The Channels

Christopher Pappas at eLearning Industry's Network suggests specific ways distance educators can use the popular social media channels to create tightly knit communities with students.

Facebook is versatile, allowing instructors to create closed or open groups for students to share information, quizzes, materials, photos, or even specific courses. Talking and commenting about shared priorities and events is easy.

Twitter can be used as a backchannel to connect learning communities and classrooms, and convey massive amounts of information via resource links to highlight courses, events, and classes. Instructors just create an account and give its hashtag to students.

LinkedIn serves as a wonderful arena for many educators across the miles to confidently share knowledge, tips, problems, and developments with qualified colleagues. Joining the Instructional Design & E-Learning Professionals' LinkedIn group is recommended.

Google+ is used heavily by both learners and facilitators because it isn't as easy to get distracted there as on Facebook and Twitter. It is a social media channel that keeps studies separate from the social context—a lot of people prefer not to mix these—and Google+ provides a way to do that through the use of "circles."

YouTube offers a special opportunity to convey teaser videos of lessons, refer students to watch videos that support in-class materials, and create mini-tip tutorials and separate coaching for students, at an individual or group level, personalizing the delivery of material.

The channels you choose are not as important as what you share on them. Meaningful content relevant and valuable to current and future students is the most important thing to give, whether it's through a blog or just a casual photo post. Following experts such as trade magazines and professional blogs can inspire you to create better content on your own pages. Hootesuite.com can help you view all your channels in one place, look for patterns in your audience's and student's needs, and collaborate with team members on group projects. This will naturally shape the products you develop. Interacting with posts is important, too. Rather than just posting something and looking at the comments people make, get invested in a meaningful conversation that can be continued in a real-life event through Meetup.com—a great place to create a real-life end of the course celebration for your students.

Human Resources

U ntil now, you've mainly been concerned about creating and displaying fantastic lesson demos, securing funding to hold you through the first two years as you build your reputation, web identity and image, proper pricing procedures, and lining up vendors, etc. Making sure you don't burn through your money before the doors are open is no doubt at the top of your priority list. Good—you're planning to succeed.

Having said that, what if you get what you want? What if you land the contract of a lifetime creating a curriculum for a new, nature-based Waldorf school for children? What if your Lawnmower Maintenance Tips and Fertilize Like a Pro videos are a smash hit with a major garden supplier and they want more of you, yesterday? Can you produce at the level that will anchor these wonderful offers? Do you really want to hold all of the

▶ Seven Tips for Hiring Smart

Be aware of these seven points from eLearning Industry on evaluating potential hires for your team:

1. *Do they have work samples?* Even newcomers to the field should have work samples to show you, even if it is just from an intern or volunteer project.

2. *Experience is as important, if not more than a degree, or skills.* Rounded real-life skills in dealing with clients, accountability, and long-term completion are honed by doing, so ask.

3. *Think about character, manners, and personality and how theirs make you feel*—it will matter in the long run when you have a stressful project, need extra tenacity on the job, and are in the spotlight.

4. *Meshing with the team is important.* New hires need to be able to feel comfortable communicating and taking direction from your team. Do they seem socially engaged and happy or concerned and challenged upon meeting your team?

5. *Are they passionate about education?* Is this the kind of person who feels excited about taking new courses and studying up on everything you have to offer? It's easy to spot a faker. Someone insincere will not have been very proactive in learning and that shows up on a resume.

6. *Is the candidate comfortable with the technology and tools you use or will the learning curve be distractingly steep?* A little bit of challenge is expected when taking a new job, but if there is no foundation, sometimes it just doesn't come together.

7. *What kind of references did they give you?* It's nice to be able to hear about how the candidate functioned on a team, overcame a challenge, completed a tough project, or went out of the way to help someone.

meetings, design all of the classes, maintain the technical aspects of the product, attend to the billing and customer communications, and create and place the marketing? Still want to do everything yourself? Can't afford to hire any help? Think again.

Hire Smart

As the quantity of work to be performed increases, you must hire employees. Elearning coach Connie Malamed (www.theelearningcoach.com) advises to hire smart. She says three people is a good starting size for a team and to manage your initial budget to its maximum potential, look at which jobs warrant only part-time hours. It's possible to turn two jobs into one with the right employee, but be careful not to overload or you may get a nasty surprise. Many employees who feel overworked keep it to themselves, feeling that if they let their

▶ Malamed's Recommendation for Building an eLearning Team

- ▶ *Project Manager*. Oversees the full life cycle of the project, interfaces between internal client and eLearning team, schedules deliverables, and ensures the team has the information and resources it needs to get the job done. Provides the business analysis to ensure that solutions are aligned with business and organizational goals.

- ▶ *Instructional Designer/Writer*. Uses instructional design, cognitive psychology, and adult learning theory to determine the appropriate solution to a knowledge or performance gap. Analyzes content, organizes content, designs solutions, and writes storyboards, scripts, performance support, mobile learning, and manuals. Knows how to use social media and collaborative tools to facilitate learning.

- ▶ *Editor*. Helps to improve overall writing; proofreads all writing

- ▶ *Graphic Designer*. Creates the user interface, graphics, and animations; designs the look and feel of courses, learning portals, mobile learning, and print materials with an eye toward the clarity required for learning and information dissemination.

- ▶ *Media Specialist*. Produces and edits audio and video when required for a project.

- ▶ *Authoring Tools Specialist*. Assembles all the elements into a running course, adds interactivity, and ensures the course can interface with an LMS, if required. With the advent of rapid tools, some instructional designers handle this role.

- ▶ *Tester*. Runs quality assurance checks by testing the course from a technical perspective and ensuring it matches the storyboard.

employer know, they'll look incapable. They fear getting fired, pay cuts, and losing prestige and responsibility.

As your company succeeds, you will need to redefine condensed job roles and divide them up into single occupations. When you start out, you will handle the lion's share, if not all, of the business functions. Small businesses often divide the work in half: You, as the owner, manage the operations, and you're assisted by someone who creates the product. As your business grows, you will probably need a project manager, operations manager, instructional designer/writer, editor, graphic designer, media specialist, authoring tools specialist, and course tester.

You don't want to wait too long before hiring a general manager to relieve you of some responsibilities. Hiring the right professional at the right time will ensure that all the jobs are getting done, which makes the business more appealing for the client and employees alike. If you are not able to get answers for customers back to your salespeople in a timely manner, this frustrates customers and costs sales.

Assessing Your Needs

The frontline employees interact with clients, so they are, in a sense, your face. You may be your own salesperson and instructional designer, and also may run your entire company. But if you don't, keep these things in mind when deciding how to staff your enterprise:

A full-time instructional designer (ID) on staff is paramount. This person should be "in the trenches through every phase of your projects," says Justin Ferriman of LearnDash (www.learndash.com). In his article "Why Every Company Must Hire an Instructional Designer," Ferriman points out that an on-staff ID becomes almost instantly indispensible after having absorbed most of the company knowledge and priorities. "Think about how much of an asset this individual immediately becomes to [the] employer. They now know the entire training program intimately from start to finish. How to edit content, where content has come from, why it exists, who the target audience is, and much more! Maintenance and quality assurance alone become much less costly to the organization because they have their own expert on-the-ground." Additional benefits to doing this are: being able to update, refresh, and keep current training materials without hiring outside help (from a noninvested source) at higher rates.

How Many People Is Enough?

The quick answer is as many as it takes to ensure complete customer satisfaction. In reality, simple economics preclude this. There are as many answers to personnel needs as there are types of training businesses. Nonetheless, here are a few points to consider in deciding how many staff members your business requires:

- ▶ *Type of business.* Is your company destined to be a *Fortune* 1000 or sole divisional learning service? Either service requires calculating production hours and dividing that by your startup budget with a reasonable allowance for profit.
- ▶ *Type of product.* The higher the price and complexity of the product, the more personal selling is required. More personal selling means more people.
- ▶ *Operating hours.* The number of workdays and the hours of business may require shifts and flexible work times. Changes in holiday business will also affect staffing.
- ▶ *Participant density.* The more students enrolled in your courses, the greater your need for trainers and more development.
- ▶ *Business location.* A homebased business increases its chances of experiencing zoning problems with every employee it adds.

Hiring

The first phase of hiring is the more impersonal aspect of personnel administration: creating plans, formulating policies, and setting up procedures. This involves recruitment, selection, hiring, compensation, employee health and welfare, maintaining personnel records, and the like. Then come the more human aspects of managing human resources—the personal, in-the-flesh people business.

A natural tendency of many new business owners is to hire family members and/or friends as soon as help is needed. Be cautious if you are thinking about doing

warning

One trainer we talked to went out on a limb to refer her casual friend to an open position in her company. This friend was new, seemed capable, and had a cheery attitude. She also seemed to be very supportive and interested in the opinions of others. The disaster occurred when shortly after she was hired she used profanity on a client, snarled at a project manager, and refused to follow instructions on a project. How could this happen and how could it have been avoided? Knowing someone for a long time or having worked with them at length on a substantial project are good ways to get a genuine feel for their character and work ethic. Many people who are eager to please to get what they want can come across as whatever they think you're looking for. Don't go out on a limb for anyone who doesn't have clout! You can jeopardize your reputation.

this. Loading your eLearning staff with "your tribe" ensures your team will be a bunch of people with a similar mindset and perhaps background, which may not be to your advantage. It's good to have a variety of thinking and learning styles at work to create a rounded product and introduce ideas you may not have cooked up on your own. The extra effort required to build good communication between co-workers can translate to honed customer communication skills.

Hiring people from your friend and family circles is also dangerous because if something goes south at home, you can be certain it will carry over into the office, even with the most professional work ethic. By the same token, if you are having a very challenging month at work, do you want your entire system of relief to be tied up there? The very friends you relish cutting loose with on weekends can turn into serious connections with too much attention paid to editing conversation and vice versa, worrying about feeling too comfortable and bringing your social sense of relaxation or sense of humor inappropriately into the workplace.

Grow your team slowly with professionals who have solid skills and experience to add to the team, and then project more work based on already having the talent to support it. It's better to stay focused and put out a steady, high-quality product, with all aspects of the client relationship covered in a breathable way than to get as much business as possible and then figure out how to do it.

Where to Find Talent

This is where any time you've spent networking can turn into gold doubloons. Just because you have a LinkedIn profile and can peruse for good candidates online doesn't mean you'll get what you need. LinkedIn is only as rich a resource as your real relationships to people on the site and the same goes for other online-based networks. There are other real life networks that function just as well as LinkedIn, so it's just best to focus on a formula, rather than which site you think has the best mining potential for employees.

The Formula: Make the Golden List

Think about the networks you're already involved in, or have been involved in, in the past, rather than suddenly joining associations and trying to grow instant solid connections. Make a list of projects on which you've worked with outstanding professionals, even if they are unrelated to your current subject matter or distance education. Add personal relationships to that list of anyone you know who is respected in her field. Next, add relevant relationships you've developed through social media connections. Think about your formal education and continuing training—there should be a lot of pros you can connect with from that source. When you've finished making a contact list of all of those important people, put the word out about the kind of skills you're looking for, in addition to the experience required to do the job. By not just focusing on the job description, you'll get a wider variety of capable people to choose from, and then you can decide if training them the rest of the way makes sense.

Networks Teaming with Talent

Networks are strong in the training industry. Educators are people who go to learning events and are frequently involved in communication; after all, these are people who thrive on stimulation. So, make a list of organizations that act as networks for trainers. Start by looking at trade journals. The list below shows just a few of many:

▶ eLearning Network (www.elearningnetwork.org)
▶ eLearning Guild (www,elearningguild.com)
▶ Training magazine (www.trainingmag.com)
▶ NYIT School of Education (www.nyit.edu)
▶ Connecticut Distance Learning Consortium (www.ctdlc.org)

When the time arrives to hire higher-level employees such as assistant managers, buyers, and bookkeepers, you need to be more imaginative and aggressive in your pursuit of qualified personnel. LinkedIn, trade journals, professional association newsletters, and relevant industry websites are good places to find seasoned, skilled, relevant prospects, often with referral status. Discussing your needs with suppliers and other educators is another way to find employees who can often hit the ground running.

Labor Practices

A person who operates a business with employees outside the immediate family must comply with a host of statutes regarding fair employment practices. These statutes relate to things like terms of employment, safety on the job, provisions for retirement, and workers' compensation and unemployment insurance. The fairness principle requires that decisions related to employees aren't made arbitrarily and that policies are applied equally to all employees. The law gives employees certain rights, and as an employer, you are responsible for knowing the law and abiding by it.

Some employees working in large companies belong to unions that represent their common interests. Consult your lawyer and SBA counselor regarding labor laws in your state.

Hiring Procedures

There are several methods for hiring and evaluating potential employees. Educate yourself on proper hiring procedures. Information on this subject is available at local libraries, community colleges, Small Business Development Centers, employment services offices, career development centers, and seminars.

tip

Great leaders keep educating themselves; so lead by example and start a book club for your employees that will light their imaginations. Create a list of dynamic reads that spark creativity and hold book club meetings during the Friday lunch hour, with a potluck option or something great to eat. Watch your regular employee meetings take off with new ideas and confidence.

Make sure your job announcement is attractive, accurate, meets government equal opportunity criteria, and is listed in the right places. Each job posting should be well thought-out to emphasize the positive aspects of the job, including benefits and potential for advancement. The medium used to advertise positions should be tailored to the job type and the type of person you hope to hire. For example, if you are looking for an experienced instructional designer, you may want to run an ad on LinkedIn.com. If you're looking for an entry-level candidate, you might be targeting writers, so advertise on in writers' forums and local writing salons or schools. You can also pass the word along to current employees to suggest friends or acquaintances, work with employment agencies, or list the opening with the state Department of Employment Services or on the web.

Some firms pay a bonus to any employee who brings in a new hire. Others spend thousands of dollars on classifieds, only to report that word-of-mouth referrals still seem to bring in the best candidates. Outstanding salespeople must be recruited, developed, and then shown they're appreciated.

It is often easier to train inexperienced people to function in a unique way in your company than to hire those seasoned in the field who have developed staff standards or habits that aren't relevant to your needs. Productivity can be developed in candidates who have a few desirable traits: friendliness, attention to detail, persistence, patience, and creativity. For example, Diane Elkins says her team at Artisan E-Learning has trained themselves much of the way. They met at those precious jobs that acted as matchmaking services for the skilled and motivated, setting them up for future project teamwork that only their imaginations set limits on. She has networked with friends and relatives and hired both and then trained them where needed. "It's just important that they have the right skill sets. I don't believe you need a master's in instructional design to work in this field. I would rather hire someone who is a clear thinker, who can organize content logically, work with subject matter experts, and organize their rambling thoughts into organized content. That person needs to be able take a jumble of information and categorize it—the same goes for folks in storyline development. It matters if they know how to use the tools and have good graphic design skills first, and we can train them for the rest."

If they're good, they have the patience and know-how to listen and work with people.

Auditioning talent can be more revealing than a series of interviews. Asking serious candidates to work on a short freelance project with your team is worth the investment of a short hire. Putting candidates through slightly stressful auditions can be an opportunity to see how well they'll perform and be able to shift gears in the future. See Figure 9–1 for information about advertising for jobs.

Sample Job Advertisement

Ad for a Trainer/Instructional Designer

Job Description

The Trainer/Instructional Designer will deliver and design training related to Company X onboarding, management development, and workforce development programs under the guidance of the Director of Learning and Talent Development. The Trainer/Instructional Designer designs adult-appropriate instructional products, materials, and programs utilizing a variety of learning platforms such as traditional instructor-led training, eLearning, job aids, paper-based or electronic manuals. Responsibilities also include planning and implementing training schedules and logistical support for identified participant groups, and publishing educational offerings to the learning management system.

Responsibilities and Standards

Plans, organizes, develops, and facilitates learning programs in response to annual plans and goals for the department and emerging needs.

Facilitates Learning and Talent Development courses and programs by serving as a credible, knowledgeable resource and creating an energizing, safe learning environment for managers and employees.

Uses appropriate methods to assess and confirm learning and performance gaps.

Researches and recommends effective instructional products, materials, and programs.

FIGURE 9–1: **Sample Job Advertisement**

Sample Job Advertisement, continued

Ensures new and existing course material is current, accurate, engaging, informative, and consistent with sound instructional design principles.

Develops and implements efficient and effective evaluation tools that measure value and impact.

Contributes to the Director of Learning and Talent Development need for oversight of program development and delivery by providing timely reports.

Coordinates the development and implementation of external content/programs with contracted providers.

Assists with pilot testing new courses and programs.

Works with the Learning and Talent Development administrative support staff to coordinate training logistics and ensure timely access to accurate course information within the online learning management system.

Oversees registration processes (online/phone/manual) for assigned learning programs/classes/activities and resources.

Maintains accurate course catalog and registration data in the online learning management system.

Provides standard reports and dashboards, and assists in creation of custom reports.

Provides for efficient, high-quality program administration within the department.

Develops action plans, timetables, benchmarks, quantitative targets for the online programs and projects in coordination with the Director of Learning and Talent Development.

Identifies and acquires necessary resources, materials, software, and skills to deliver services and projects.

Delivers projects on time and to agreed-upon standards, including updates and issues identification.

Creates and maintains strong working relationships with corporate and affiliate administrative and instructor groups.

Partners with corporate and affiliate administrators to identify needs and enhancements for learning programs.

FIGURE 9–1: **Sample Job Advertisement,** continued

Sample Job Advertisement, continued

Collaborates and communicates with corporate and affiliate developers, instructional designers, and system administrators to support effective use of Learning and Talent Development courses and resources.

Provides opportunities for learning and knowledge sharing across the corporate and affiliate administrative and instructor groups.

Supports professional standards for learning and performance.

Assists the Director of Learning and Talent Development/Chief Learning Officer in the development, implementation, interpretation, and evaluation of program standards, policies, procedures, and best practices to collaboratively meet the needs of managers and employees

Desired Qualifications and Experience

Bachelor's Degree in Instructional Design, Adult Education, Organization Development, Human Resources, Business, or a related field required.

Professional training or instructional design certification is a plus.

Minimum of four years' professional experience in a combination of training, workplace learning, or management consulting.

Desired Skills

Strong presentation and facilitation skills with both small and large groups

Solid experience with onboarding/orientation, management development, and workplace development programs

Strong skills in instructional design principles, instructional technologies, and adult learning

Strong skills in planning, facilitation, interviewing, research, client communications, and report/presentation writing

Good program, project, and team management skills with the ability to manage enterprise wide implementations across diverse organizations

Strong productivity application skills, including proficiency with Microsoft Office products (including Outlook, PowerPoint, and Project)

Experience with eLearning authoring tools (Articulate, Storyline, Captivate) and learning management systems (Halogen eLearning a plus)

FIGURE 9–1: **Sample Job Advertisement,** continued

Sample Job Advertisement, continued

Effective communicator to senior-level training and business management with a good pragmatic approach to learning interventions and strong "results focus"

High-performance orientation with understanding of current learning industry best practices

Ablility to meet deadlines, strong organizational/time management skills, and execution-focused

Self-directed with the ability to assimilate large amounts of information quickly and capable of keeping pace with fast-changing learning technology industry

To be considered for this position, email a cover letter and resume to HR@CompanyXYZ.com.

FIGURE 9–1: **Sample Job Advertisement,** continued

Background Checks

There is no crystal ball to ensure that the employees you hire will be loyal, honest, and hard-working. It is wise to screen applicants more thoroughly than simply asking them to fill out a job application and calling a few of the person's friends. Since everyone from the content developer to the IT staff represents your business, you should either verify an applicant's background or hire someone to do it for you.

Howtoinvestigate.com is an online organization that outlines information sources and procedures for you to accomplish a background check. Local investigation firms can also be found in your town with a simple Google search, as well as through your police department and lawyers association. They will do background criminal checks on prospective employees for about $50 to $250, depending on the agency's fee schedule and how many jurisdictions the agency checks.

Verifying Employment Eligibility

Employers must have proof that the employee has the right to work in the country, as required on U.S.

warning

Both students and trainers must be aware of diploma mills and fake certifications. Students don't want to lose their money and time, and trainers don't want to hire someone from a school with phony accreditations. To check out the validity of a school, go to Diploma Mill Police at Get Educated to search its list of distance learning reports, scams, and diploma mills here: www.geteducated.com/ diploma-mill-police/ degree-mills-list.

Citizenship and Immigration Service (USCIS) Form I–9. To learn about the requirements your business must meet view: uscis.gov/working-united-states/information-employers-employees/employer-information. View acceptable identity and authorization to work documents here: uscis.gov/i-9-central/acceptable-documents.

New employees must provide you with either one document from List A (Identity and Employment Authorization) or one document each from Lists B (Identity only) and C (Employment Authorization only):

List A

▶ U.S. Passport or U.S. Passport Card

▶ Permanent Residence Card or Alien Registration Receipt Card

▶ Foreign Passport with I–551 stamp or temporary I–551 printed notation on machine-readable immigrant visa (MRIV)

▶ Employment Authorization Document card with photograph (Form I–766)

▶ Foreign Passport with Form I–94 or Form I–94A with Arrival/Departure Report bearing same name on passport with endorsement of nonimmigrant status and specific work endorsement

▶ Passport from the Federated States of Micronesia (FSM) or the Republic of the Marshall Island (RMI) with From I–94 or Form I–94A showing nonimmigrant admission under the Compact of Free Association Between the U.S. and the FSM or RMI

▶ Foreign passport with special documents issued by the Commonwealth of Northern Mariana Island (CNMI)

▶ Foreign passport that contains a temporary I–551 stamp or temporary I–551 printed notation on a machine readable immigrant visa (MRIV)

List B

▶ Driver's license or ID card issued by a state or outlying possession of the United States with a photograph, date of birth, physical description, and address

▶ School identification card with photograph

▶ Voter's registration card

▶ U.S. military card or draft record

▶ Military dependent's ID card

▶ U.S. Coast Guard Merchant Mariners Document (MMD)

▶ Native American tribal document

▶ Driver's license issued by Canadian authority

▶ Acceptable List B documents for those under 18

- ▶ School record or report card
- ▶ Clinical, doctor, or hospital record
- ▶ Day-care or nursery school record

See www.uscis.gov for special notations that can be used in place of these for the disabled or minors who are unable to produce these documents.

List C

- ▶ U.S. Social Security account number card that is unrestricted
- ▶ Certification of Birth Abroad issued by the U.S. Department of State (Form FS–545)
- ▶ Certification of Report of Birth issued by the U.S. Department of State (Form DS–1350)
- ▶ Original or certified copy of birth certificate issued by a state, county, municipal authority, or outlying possession of the United States bearing an official seal
- ▶ Native American Tribal document
- ▶ U.S. Citizen ID card (Form I–197)
- ▶ Identification Card for Use of Resident Citizen in the United States (Form I–179)
- ▶ Employment authorization document issued by the Department of Homeland Security (see www.uscis.gov for details).

Employee Compensation

According to the U.S. Department of Labor's 2014 tally, there are 133,780 instructional coordinators working across the U.S. today. Their average annual salary is $64,040 and their average hourly rate is $30.79. They develop instructional material, coordinate educational content, and incorporate current technology in specialized fields that provide guidelines to educators and instructors for developing curricula and conducting courses. They also act as educational consultants and specialists, and instructional material directors. Because this occupation requires a lot of flexibility and skill sets, it is a good sampling of what it is like to work in distance learning. The average weekly earnings of all full-time wage and salary workers in every profession combined were $784 in the first quarter of 2014, compared to the weekly instructional coordinator earnings of $1,231. Note that though the average salary is $64,040, 90 percent of instructional coordinators made $95,590, and 10 percent $37,000.

Most full-time employees expect health coverage, paid time off for illness or vacation, and some perks like paid educational opportunities, trade show attendance, and product or service discounts. Without offering some benefits in your compensation package, you will find it difficult to compete for quality employees. When considering what to offer your workers, compare the perks with the costs of high turnover—decreased morale, time interviewing new employees, training new people, interruption of customer service, public perception of instability, loss of person's know-how, etc.

After They're Hired

Once you have invested the time and effort in recruiting and hiring skilled new employees, don't rest on your laurels. Your work's not done! There are several things you can do to ensure your diligent hiring efforts don't go to waste.

Lack of communication between management and employees is a big mistake and all too common. Don't let your business fall into this common trap. Regular company meetings are a good way to improve the situation. These gatherings are great settings for educating employees on new products or services. Let an employee explain and demonstrate benefits and features of your products. Have employees tell you what

▶ Do What it Takes to Keep Your Team Happy

Care about how your staff feels. It's important to be a leader and to push and challenge your team, but if you have unrealistic expectations and only care about the end result, your product, you are not only being selfish, you're also being careless about your talent investment. You may find that after never hearing so much as a peep of frustration, your employees are quitting, and have other jobs lined up. Follow these tips to keep your flock from fleeing:

▶ *Pay them what they're worth*. Look up salary averages for your area and match them. Don't underpay or you'll foster growing resentment.

▶ *Reward and acknowledge achievements*, whether it is with a gift certificate or bonus.

▶ *Find out what's both relevant to company growth and personally important to employees and support those goals as best you can*. Investing in upgrading employee training always makes them feel valued and when personal goals intersect with what's good for the company, you have a smart investment.

▶ *Hold one-to-one meetings with each employee every six months or more often*. Ask how they feel about potential obstacles, where they are going, if they have the help they need to complete projects, and what they are excited about. If you only get answers designed for Brownie points, ask, "Just between you and me, honestly, what would you change about your role here if you could change anything?"

features or products they observe customers liking or disliking and what they hear customers asking for that may not be ready to release. Employees should be told about new developments in the curriculum and want to be asked for their opinions and see some of their ideas implemented.

Provide Incentives to Employees

Employees should constantly be encouraged to perform in a quality manner. When you or a customer is pleased with an employee's performance, let everyone know about it. Personal and public recognition has a multitiered affect. It communicates what you value to your workers and customers, which can generate more achievements and satisfaction. Some rewards the companies we interviewed use are treating a star employee to a lunch, bonus, afternoon off, or reserved parking. You will be hiring from the same labor pool as other local businesses. How can you get your employees to perform better for you? Your acknowledgment, rewards, and overall management will make all the difference.

▶ The Employee Bible

Here are some of the topics you should cover in your employee manual:

- ▶ Company philosophy and mission
- ▶ Company benefits, including medical care, time off, discounts, and allowances
- ▶ Hours of operation and reporting hours
- ▶ Procedures for reporting an illness, absence, or family emergency
- ▶ Dress code
- ▶ Standards of behavior regarding smoking, alcohol, drugs, gum-chewing, language, personal telephone calls, and visitors
- ▶ How to communicate with clients
- ▶ Telephone etiquette
- ▶ Procedures for resolving product malfunctions
- ▶ Procedures for dealing with unhappy clients
- ▶ Procedures for making suggestions for company improvement
- ▶ How to use all software and equipment, and training procedures
- ▶ Where to get product or service information
- ▶ Emergency procedures

Employee and Operations Manual

Operating a training business can be very gratifying and stimulating, but without effective management procedures, it can also be a lot of headaches. If you put the proper systems in place so that your store is more or less on autopilot, you'll be successful. The reason franchises generally work well is that they use proven systems; all the new operator has to do is follow the tried-and-true policies.

An employee and operations manual provides the information your people need to do their jobs and play by the rules. It gets employees off on the right foot and instills in them habits you want to see rather than those you want to break.

Many trainers are extremely dependent on their key staff members. If a management person leaves, sales suffer because of the knowledge that walks out the door with a valuable employee. Turnover is expensive, and training new staff is a tedious, time-consuming process. Written operating procedures that explain how to perform the day-to-day, week-to-week, month-to-month, and year-to-year jobs involved in running your store will help smooth employee transitions.

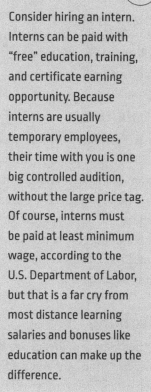

aha!

Consider hiring an intern. Interns can be paid with "free" education, training, and certificate earning opportunity. Because interns are usually temporary employees, their time with you is one big controlled audition, without the large price tag. Of course, interns must be paid at least minimum wage, according to the U.S. Department of Labor, but that is a far cry from most distance learning salaries and bonuses like education can make up the difference.

By having a guide for employees, you eliminate uncertainty about what your company's policies, procedures, and guidelines are. This can be of particular importance when you need to put an employee on probation or fire someone. Clearly stated policies can protect you from the litigation that is all too common in today's world.

For the most part, the educated professionals you'll attract to your team will not need to be informed of a dress code, and the casual corporate style most smaller companies go with today is simply a look that is tidy, comfortable, and respectable. But if for some reason you have a great team member who doesn't have a clue about personal hygiene or too revealing clothing, it's a smart idea to have had them review your basic decorum or style standards agreement, rather than subjecting everyone to a dress code. Clients are influenced by every personality in your company and judgments can be made quickly about your entire organization based on just a small detail, such as chipped nail polish or stained clothing.

Managing the client's mood is not a small task. Management of the client experience starts with the first point of contact. A warm greeting from an alert, knowledgeable, and attentive (but not pushy) salesperson will make customers want to do business with you time and again.

Probation

It is customary to hire new people on a probationary basis. This period should be relatively short—for example, 10 to 90 days. This time allows you to evaluate the new employee to measure their progress and to determine if they will fit into your organization. A probationary period also provides incentive for new employees to prove themselves and to learn their jobs quickly and well.

Training

When new employees are hired, they should be trained in a well-thought-out and thorough manner. To begin orienting them to your way of doing business, give them a complete tour of the facilities, explaining what their role is in each area, what procedures to follow, and things to watch out for. Take new employees through the entire company from the front door to the back. It is important that everyone understand how their job fits into the overall scheme of things and what each person's duties and responsibilities are so people will work well together.

tip

Make sure to give the new hire a bio and contact list to refer to, containing each member of your staff, their title and role in the organization, and their contact information. If you don't already have one of these, then make one, and if it has photos, so much the better. If employee bios are listed on your website, refer the employee there. This will give an understanding of how the whole system works and shorten the learning curve, making the new hire feel more comfortable and able to focus on the work. Make sure all employees are on the list and that it is complete and updated regularly.

Continue training on a regular basis. Training is an investment in the future—your future. With rapid changes in technology and the psychology of learning, products change frequently and the challenge to employees to keep up with them is great.

Encourage employees to stay informed about the latest trends in your industry by reading trade journals and industry news. Send employees to trade and consumer shows to pick up new ideas, interact with other businesspeople, and promote your business.

Scheduling Personnel

Scheduling employee hours when you first start might be challenging until you really have a feel for how long it takes to create and manage each product, but as you schedule for each project, and perhaps begin with on-call contractors, you'll know what is required when you start operating at a higher, more consistent level.

Full-time employees work 30 to 40 hours a week and are usually paid at a somewhat higher hourly rate than part-time employees (or they are paid salary). Full-timers provide continuity for your business and help develop your customer base for you. They generally have multifaceted skills in many areas of training and education. They may have a little IT, a lot of writing, some content development, and other bits of experience. These employees make a commitment to your business and have regularly scheduled hours and days of the week.

Part-time employees may work year-round or with increased hours when you need extra help. They can be scheduled for your heavy-traffic hours and days or on an as-needed basis. These workers are frequently students, retired people, or parents of school-age children, and their schedules can be set to accommodate school and/or seasonal schedules. Establishing four-hour shifts allows you the flexibility of having people work partial days as well as adjusting staffing needs. Some of your part-time workers will stay with you for years and provide exceptional service.

Invite employees to submit schedule requests and make every effort to accommodate them. However, don't be casual on the accountability side. Let employees know you are counting on them and expect them to arrive on time and ready to work. Overstaffing, understaffing, and no-shows disrupt other workers and can jeopardize your business. By maintaining detailed sales, traffic, and staffing records, you can analyze what's working and what isn't. From year to year, you'll amass figures that will help you maximize your resources and opportunities.

Employee Performance Appraisals

Annual employee evaluations help you zero in on the strengths and weaknesses of your business. At the same time each year, set up appointments with your employees to review their performance. Give each employee a self-evaluation form to complete and return to you prior to your scheduled meeting. Then, review each employee's answers and prepare your points for discussion. These will include expectations for the job, personal achievements, areas where effectiveness could improve, how you can help the employee do a better job, and the employee's new performance objectives.

From the information exchanged during the performance appraisal process, you will get a clearer view of how well your hiring, training, and management practices are working. You will also gain insight into ways to motivate employees. This is often a time when new ideas for the business surface and aspirations for promotion are revealed. Performance appraisals also provide the opportunity for clearing the air about misunderstandings or mistakes and for starting fresh.

The laws protecting workers' rights are complex and can easily be used against you. Check with your lawyer, local Small Business Development Center, and other advisors to ensure you understand what you can and cannot do in terms of firing an employee.

If you feel you need to discipline an employee, the first thing you need to do is meet with the employee and give him or her a verbal warning. The next time the employee exhibits behavior that goes against your policies, meet with the employee and provide him or her with a written summary of things the employee must and must not do and a time period within which the employee must correct his or her performance. This is known as a written warning. Keep a copy of the warning that clearly states that if the behavior is not corrected, the employee may be terminated. Ask the employee to sign the warning, acknowledging the understanding of your expectations. If, after these measures, the employee's performance has not improved in the ways you outlined in the verbal and written warnings, you may have to fire the employee.

Be humane if you have to let someone go. Meet in private with the employee and tell the person the exact reasons for termination. Create an atmosphere of fairness, if not compassion, and have the employee's final paycheck and paperwork ready to make a clean break.

aha!

Unless an employee steals, destroys property, or causes safety problems, immediate dismissal for poor performance isn't a good idea— legally or managerially. Communicate in a gentle, clear way, what is going wrong and how to correct it. Create a written record of these communications in the unfortunate event that the employee chooses to ignore the criticisms. You need a paper trail to show proper procedures were taken, and fair opportunity to improve was given, if you have to fire someone.

Give
Great
Content

You can either create your own content or buy it. In either case, it has to be relevant to the learner. This is why you should be sure to work hard to define your audience, including conducting surveys and focus groups and paying attention to the results.

The first thing to do to get your hands on great content is write down what your objectives are, rather than focus on the information you want to convey (e.g., "help people become safer drivers" rather than "the faster your speed, the greater distance you should leave between you and the car in front of you"). Second, make sure that your objectives are really what your market wants to learn. Third, you need to understand how it will be using the new knowledge, because that may change what you teach, the way you teach it, and how long you make it. For example, if your objective is to make it easier for employees of a lawn care products company to convey information to customers about your products, then ask them how long they typically talk with customers and what their most asked questions are. Then you can build a short content product that delivers the answers to the most asked questions the customers have in a short time frame.

Your content should give no more and no less information to the employees who need it and let them test their knowledge quickly. For the lawn care scenario, your interface should be designed for mobile apps because employees will likely be roving the store and need information on the fly; they'll also probably be taking your short courses in-between doing other things. Finally, analyze whether the content you have planned accomplishes your shared objectives with the customer. Before launching the product use a test group of real salespeople and ask them if it solves their problems.

Your Class Must Match Program Goals

Just because you know your subject doesn't mean it will be a snap to write your coursework. It's important to structure an outline for what you will teach, with enough room to demonstrate a clear path to how learning objectives will be achieved. Whether you are designing your classes to train clients independently or writing a proposal to be accepted as a staff member at a teaching facility, you must clearly show how your class matches the goals of the existing program. If you are designing smaller, light tutorials as an add-on service or benefit to your business, be sure you clearly define how they support your business and what need they fill. Figure 10–1 on page 145 can help you plan.

In developing her syllabus, Schuh had to rethink how she structured her ideas. "In designing workshops I was accustomed to outlining activities more so than learning objectives. For the university I was challenged to more closely consider teaching outcomes—what the students were expected to do upon completion of the course. For example, following eight weeks of study they would ideally be able to identify their beliefs, fears, experiences, and attitudes that influence equanimity and anxiety surrounding their own mortality. And if I were successful in teaching the students, they would be able to implement a plan to ultimately assure congruence with their unique vision of a life well lived. These are just two of several intended objectives."

Course Content Worksheet

1. Start your learning objective process by asking how you want the student to have changed as a result of the new knowledge. Consider some of the assignments Schuh used to accomplish and measure the results. _____

   _____

   _____

2. What is the goal of your class? Why do you think it's important? To whom will it matter most? Define your demographic. _____

   _____

3. What problems will your class solve for the learner? _____

   _____

4. Write three sentences that demonstrate how you want learners to have changed as a result of taking your class. _____

   _____

   _____

   _____

5. What will they be able to do better than before? _____

   _____

6. What tools will they be able to use, or what skills will they have developed? _____

   _____

7. What new questions may they have? _____

8. What textbooks, videos, or other learning materials will help teach your class? _____

   _____

9. Explain why each delivery method will be used for that segment of your class. Make sure there is a good reason for each delivery method you choose. _____

   _____

FIGURE 10–1: **Course Content Worksheet**

Course Content Worksheet, continued

10. Will there be a mix of synchronous and asynchronous lessons, or interactions? List them and explain why. _____

_____

_____

11. How will students show you they've learned or achieved the set learning objectives? What tests or assignments will be used to measure this? _____

_____

_____

_____

_____

FIGURE 10–1: **Course Content Worksheet,** continued

Schuh helped her students achieve these outcomes and demonstrate their insights, conclusions, and resolves by requiring them to:

▶ Create a confidential online journal that captures their responses to specific queries posted weekly.

▶ Use personal reflections to react to assigned reading material (by writing in the journal).

▶ View specific TED Talks and thoughtfully respond to their related posted queries.

▶ Dialog with classmates on the discussion board.

▶ Summarize their collective epiphanies surrounding the study of mortality in an in-depth paper to demonstrate their understanding.

Syllabus Development

Students will expect a syllabus, or outline, of the class at the beginning. Your syllabus should include class dates, in-class curriculum on those dates, assignments and their due dates, dates of any quizzes and tests, as well as reading assignments. The syllabus should include what is expected of the students to receive each grade level or pass/fail designation for the class.

How the Brain Learns

We've all experienced the brain-dead syndrome while studying something that doesn't seem interesting but we have to learn it. The information seems to go on forever but we can't absorb it and then, as if by magic, we begin reading or hearing something that truly interests us and find we can recite the whole thing backward and forward just from a few minutes of totally engrossed exposure.

The onus is on you to find ways to make the dull information more interesting! If you can find captivating methods for teaching the most mundane information, students will flock to your classes. On the other hand, you also have to be careful to ensure the presentation of your material does not make it seem less important. This is where the use of gaming techniques for online coursework can be extremely useful and worth investing in the expertise to help you create such a curriculum approach. More on gaming techniques below.

Motivate, Capture, Personalize

Use opening statements, questions, and statistics that demand a dramatic response. Demonstrate why the information should matter to the student. Show them how their lives will be different and what they'll be able to do better after the course. Use real-life examples of how this has already happened. These opening communications should be like the first few pages of a gripping mystery—it should be impossible to not go forward. Set their imaginations loose to run wild.

Be a Master Storyteller

Use as many dramatic, funny, or entertaining stories as you can to convey your material. People remember stories and retain their information longer than dryly-presented facts.

Use Striking Images and Infographics

Illustration of the concepts you are teaching always helps. A picture, as the saying goes, truly can be worth a thousand words. If you find your lesson is droning on and on with boring text, think through whether a graphic or image might better convey your message. It is worth whatever you need to pay for the graphic (be sure not to just use photos and graphics without permission—just because it is on the internet does not make it free for general use).

Cartoons can be great for getting concepts across. Again, if you find the perfect cartoon online, be sure to ask permission to use it. Many cartoonists can be hired to do work specifically for your content at a reasonable fee.

Chunking

There are reasons phone numbers are grouped into small sections. We have a greater chance of memorizing the small sections than the whole jumble of numbers at once. Giving learners only a paragraph or two at a time to read is especially important on a computer, which strains the eyes and competes with easy distractions like surfing the internet and checking email.

Procession Graphics

These are the clickable icons or text that the learner uses to advance the page. Out with the old and in with the new. Getting rid of material already read and only seeing new material gives a sense of accomplishment and confidence, as does seeing the accomplished modules or sections below the lesson, and how many are left. Being able to move backward and staying on a page as long as they want allows readers to customize their learning. This is one of the reasons self-paced learning is achieving higher absorption rates online, in addition to relieving the stress associated with having to "hurry up and learn!"

Summarize, Summarize, Summarize

Small groupings of information should be together in the chunking method we just mentioned. After each section, the learner should get a summary or bullet list of the key learning points. This reinforces the important parts of the information and ensures absorption.

Turn It into a Game

Part of the testing process can be turned into a game. Gamification is a huge trend in eLearning right now because it is fun, helps learners stay focused on the material, and has measurable results. Did you get eaten by the dragon or didn't you? Here are some websites that do it well:

> ▶ *Nursing Simulation* (www.suddenlysmart.com/examples/Patient_Management/player.html). Screen patients and recommend treatment.

▶ *Crash Scene Investigation* (www.edheads.org/activities/crash_scene). Use trigonometry, physics, and geometry to process a deadly crime scene.

▶ *CameraSim* (www.camerasim.com). This recreation of a digital single lens reflex camera teaches users how to use one.

▶ *Design a Cell Phone* (www.edheads.org/activities/eng_cell). Analyze market research to build the perfect cell phone.

Test Their Thinking Frequently

Following a series of multiple-choice questions, and before the actual testing, give them frequent opportunities to give answers in short composition-style bursts. Asking them to convey their understanding in writing re-exposes them to the lesson and having to write it reinforces it to memory. You can give some guidelines to help coach them, such as showing some sample answers or restricting answers to three sentences, etc. Hint boxes can be available to click if they need them.

Blended Learning

"Blended learning" refers to the combination of instructional delivery via in-class situations and online learning. Depending upon what kind of eLearning business you are creating, this might be something you could incorporate. Or perhaps you could do this with a specific class that you can teach both in your community and online and use the physical classroom setting for useful face-to-face interaction and feedback gathering about your class.

The Perfect Synchronous/Asynchronous Salad

While many classes are either completely synchronous with everyone in the class sitting down at their computer at the same time or completely asynchronous where students take the entire class on their own schedule, a combination of the two can make an online class much more interesting for students. The topic of your class and the typical student that might be taking that class will determine how much synchronous class time is enough. Many students are drawn to eLearning specifically because it is flexible, so don't make your class so inflexible with specific class time that you turn away your core potential students.

Design It for Cell Phones

Cell phones have become the tablet-of-choice for many people, especially the younger generation. Smartphones are becoming bigger and bigger to accommodate this life between the traditional compact cell phone and the tablet computer. Keep in mind that many of your students are taking classes online because they have busy schedules and are on the go a lot. eLearning fits into their busy lives. An entire industry is built around creating mobile-device-friendly versions of websites. Make sure you are on that bandwagon—it isn't just a fad, it is real life.

Study What Fails

Course content that is dated or hard to understand is distracting and erodes confidence in the teacher. Your content should at the least be proofed by a subject matter expert (SME) and focus group tested. Ineffective objectives lead to ineffective results. According to LearnDash (www.learndash.com), you should consider this before writing yours:

► The multiple objectives for the entire initiative; high-level or end-game objectives, course objectives, and individual lesson objectives.

► Seven Low-Cost Certifications to Plump Your Resume

Many of the free classes at www.edX.org offered by major universities can help you get started as a great trainer. You may earn low-cost Verified Certificates of Achievement for most classes on the site, and that'll look great on your resume:

Classes	Duration	Time Required
1. Building Mobile Experiences, MIT	12 weeks	10–12 hours per week
2. Creating a Course, edX	self-paced	
3. Design and Development of Games for Learning, MIT	9 weeks	6–10 hours per week
4. Design and Development of Educational Technology, MIT	13 weeks	4–6 hours per week
5. Introduction to Game Design, MIT	6 weeks	8–10 hours per week
6. Leaders of Learning, Harvard	6 weeks	4–6 hours per week
7. The Art of Teaching, GEMS	3 weeks	6–7 hours per week

▶ Sequence and order are important in the planning stage. Each objective accomplishes the one above it, and lesson objectives should assist in accomplishing the course objective. Course objectives satisfy a program objective.

▶ Students should be clear about the takeaways.

Verified Certificates of Achievement

EdX, the "nonprofit online initiative created by founding partners Harvard and MIT," launched a Verified Certificate of Achievement. This document is for a list of eligible courses that, for a fee, provides verification of your identity and completion of the course. It enables students to provide proof to potential employers or current employers offering a promotion that they have taken the course work. Think of it as the online official transcript, one course at a time.

Keep in mind that edX courses are free. While students can still have proof of their participation in a class, the verification process provides a proof that students can show with their certificate.

Think about certificates for your classes if you feel this would enhance your marketability. Self-enrichment classes do not need this level of certification but classes that might result in employment promotion/raises or even employment itself can be more desirable with certification.

Marketing

You need to expose your business to gaps in the market, knowledge-hungry audiences, and accidental customers—those who weren't looking for you but could consider you invaluable after they know about you. Here are some ways to do that.

Start with What You've Got

Utilizing a network you already have is a start for creating a bigger one. You can take a few connections and turn them into hundreds, with work. If you went to a vocational school after high school, consider remarketing yourself to that school as a virtual trainer for their current students, especially if you've excelled in what you learned there and can contribute in the field knowledge that might not be learned in the classroom. Go back to past employers who were happy with your work and tell them what you're doing. Ask if they know anyone who could lend support to your efforts. Calling a trade association and asking for short, informational interviews with the heads of the organization can lead to connections to other people and great advice. Sending out a newsletter to friends and family announcing your goals can unearth new connections.

Passive and Active Marketing

Passive and active marketing are two different ways to show the world what you're doing that achieve very different results. Passive marketing includes market researching places and people to put advertising in front of, calculating and creating the ads, then connecting them to planned entities like mailing lists and specialized audiences. Some examples of this are:

- ▶ Print ads for magazines, newspapers, and trade publications
- ▶ Digital ads for websites with like-minded services or products
- ▶ Radio spots aired when and where your target audience listens
- ▶ TV commercials aired during programs your target audience watches
- ▶ Coupons sent to customers already involved in some aspect of your industry
- ▶ Online directory or phone book ads
- ▶ Paid advertising on sites like Yelp, YouTube, and Facebook
- ▶ Fliers and one-page info sheets for distribution through other businesses or at events
- ▶ Video demos of your product on YouTube or websites you have a relationship with
- ▶ Offering freebies as lead generation on your social media site and website

Some of the benefits of passive marketing are that it can be done on your own time, in your own way, and requires less social energy. Giving presentations requires a number of steps like getting to the event, lots of small talk and remembering names, being cheerful and "on stage," being prepared for any question, being armed with promotional materials, and dressing impeccably. Passive advertising just requires that you create the ads, or have them created, send them to the right places, keep track of analytics, and act on those results.

Active marketing is about engaging with people face-to-face and harkens back to the days when salespeople or tradesmen went from village to village, talking up their wares. They had conversations with people in each town about how their products would function in unique situations and how they could help the client. Often people would gather around in a town square and the peddler would put on a show, dramatizing the effects of the miracle product. They only had a short time to get their message across so they made the most of it, calling up nonbelievers to the stage and demonstrating with showy results to make the crowd gasp in wonder. After the crowd was hooked they'd talk about a special deal with some sort of commitment: "Buy two now and get the third free."

Though snake oil is not your game and your distance learning offerings are nothing if not honest, holding this old timey method of storytelling and presentation in your mind as you move forward is wise. Think about only having one opportunity to tell your story with each new audience you get in front of to make the most of the words you choose, the tools you use, and the way you use your personality to plant seeds in their minds.

One of the biggest benefits to active marketing is immediate feedback. There in the faces of your audience you see how they feel, whether they laugh at your jokes, whether they are rapt in your fascinating content, or if they check their cell phones over and over as you present. You don't get this with passive marketing. You only know if the viewer took your bait and where they hopped off the boat. Another benefit is removing several steps of communication if someone is interested. If you're at an event and someone likes what you do, they may approach you and talk about it as opposed to sending out a mailer, waiting for calls, playing phone tag and then taking a few discussions to determine if the potential client really wants what they think you have.

Another benefit is that you are delivering a memorable experience to the audience that passive marketing cannot, and if done right, at a fraction of the cost.

Some examples of active marketing are:

- ▶ *Focus groups made up customers you already have*, or a select group of your target demographic
- ▶ *On-site, impromptu promotion.* This could happen at a seminar you are conducting and be accidental when a client asks a question that leads to you further investigating and promoting a new solution on the spot.
- ▶ *Bringing an event to a customer.* This could be something like creating an app for a party or event that engages people and teaches them something quickly.
- ▶ *Speaking to a group for educational purposes* and gifting them your knowledge.
- ▶ *Holding an event through Meetup.com.* Find your target audience "club" and treat them to something special that both helps them and showcases what you do. An

example of this would be hosting a webinar in person for a group of writers or parents, if you teach writing or teen education.

► *Offer your products for a prize for a contest or charity auction.*

Finding Your Audience

You might be wondering whom you should invite to these wonderful presentations, and whom you should focus on for your passive marketing. Creating a list of your core potential customers involves looking hard at what you do and creating branches to everyone connected to it. Not everyone you target will function as a direct customer. Many people may solely be supporters and promoters of your business.

When deciding what the balance of active and passive marketing for your business should be, consider what each will generate for you, how long it will take to work, and how much money you have to sustain it.

► Consider This One-Hour-a-Day Formula

Mathematician Richard W. Hamming's (1915–1998) speech "You and Your Research" gives insights into what it takes to develop society-changing contributions over a lifetime. The idea expressed below can be applied to any field where complex problems are to be solved and discoveries are to be made. Through the speech he paraphrased great lessons he'd learned from colleagues. At one point in his career, Hamming was jealous of a colleague and said,

"How can anybody my age know as much as John Tukey does?" His boss, mathematician Hendrik Wade Bode, said, "You would be surprised, Hamming, how much you would know if you worked as hard as he did that many years." Hamming took it to heart and formed the work ethic he illustrates below. Take this concept seriously if you want to make a major discovery or contribution, and be miles ahead of the pack.

"Knowledge and productivity are like compound interest. Given two people of approximately the same ability and one person who works 10 percent more than the other, the latter will more than twice out-produce the former. The more you know, the more you learn; the more you learn, the more you can do; the more you can do, the more the opportunity—it is very much like compound interest. I don't want to give you a rate, but it is a very high rate. Given two people with exactly the same ability, the one person who manages day in and day out to get in one more hour of thinking will be tremendously more productive over a lifetime."

If you choose to use a combination of several of these methods, remember that your ads and presentations should convey a consistency with your brand, and with one another. Each method should contain an action step and a way to track if that is working and what the return on your investment is: "Buy 10 lessons now and receive a 3-hour personal tutor session by clicking here." To track whether the rise in business you see is because of this ad, you can assign a tracking URL to the "Click Here" button to that campaign on your site as well as use a different phone number for it.

Lesson Number One: Sing Your Song

Tie your shoes and start marching! Really. Get off the couch and make a list of the face-to-face experiences that will enhance your business in the areas of teamwork, exposure, funding, and further development. Active marketing is about getting in front of people with your ideas, needs, and identity. It's about creating a valid presence in your community, which can extend beyond your city and state to include the community of educators all over the U.S. in your niche area. Some examples of active marketing are:

▶ Create a series of short demo videos that capture the essence of your curriculum and a presentation that conveys your mission. Take it to schools, corporations, and industry networking functions.

▶ Create When You're Creative—What?

The science of creativity is a complex one, but scientists who study the creative process have identified some of the key elements that allow great ideas to come up through the mind, into a place where we can access, make sense of, and use them. Consider the following factors the next time you're creating a marketing pitch, designing a lesson, or just hoping for new inspiration.

Dopamine, a brain chemical that helps you feel bliss, focus, and motivation, is influenced by factors that you can control. While this is not a direct health recommendation, as we are not doctors, we think it's prudent to understand the power your body and actions have on your brain to be the smartest, most highly functioning entrepreneur you can be. Getting eight or more hours of undisturbed sleep per night, exercising at least 30 minutes per day, decreasing sugar and caffeine, removing stress from your life, and correcting a magnesium deficiency can help increase dopamine. Read more about what you can do to balance healthy brain chemistry at Natural Health Advisory (www.naturalhealthadvisory.com).

▶ Write an article that features your work as a tool that solves a problem. If your product is an app that teaches people how to make healthy food in ten minutes or less, add a 60-second video clip to your article and send it out to a parenting and health-conscious demographic. Yoga studios, fitness-training associations, after-school programs, and libraries would be good places to present.

Relaxation

Alpha waves in the brain increase when we relax, as in really relax, not sit in a hammock stressing about all the work we are not getting done. As we relax, our brains can unwind and reframe a problem without the threat of disaster if we choose the wrong solution or get it done fast enough. Some ideas for increasing alpha waves include meditation, yoga, biofeedback training (read more at www.mayoclinic.com using the search box), and binaural beats (read more here: www.binauralbrains.com; and listen to free beats here: www.mynoise.net/noiseMachines.php). Read *The New York Times* article, "Relax! You'll Be More Productive" by Tony Schwartz, at www.nytimes.com.

Capture

Great minds report getting some of their best ideas while doing other things, like sleeping, exercising, showering, or driving. Keep a notebook or tablet with you at all times or learn how to use voice memo on your smartphone—pull the car over or jump out of the shower to record your jewels before they fade away. Try to use the same notebook rather than stashing several in opportune places. This will help you see the progression of your ideas and be able to organize them into something fully usable like a presentation.

Presentations

Carl Tyson attributes a large part of Thinkwell's development success to telling people about the company concept. Seems simple, right? You have this great idea, you try to attract team members to help develop it, you seek investors through some research and networking—but something's missing. Really, when you put your ideas to work in a traditional mission statement or advertising spot you are just selling the part of your idea that wants money. What you need to do is sell your passion, sell the enthusiasm that made you fall head over heels with your business idea.

In each step of the development process it's important to find an audience of people with similar interests and tell them what you are doing. Just being you and loving what you are doing isn't enough. You need to get up on a stage and present your life's work as the dramatic theater piece that it is. After all, if your idea is spectacular enough for you to devote the coming years of your life to, then doesn't it stand to reason that others could be as excited as you are? Conveying why your idea needs to come to life—or if it's already moving ahead at full speed, then why it needs to grow— is as important as nurturing friendships in your personal life. Interacting with peers multiplies everything: chances for success, funding, business opportunities, growth, and rich development.

In a way, your marketing efforts should parallel your quest for financing and building a team, and the three can sometimes be accomplished together. Presenting your idea at conferences like South By Southwest (SXSW, see www.sxswedu.com) in Austin, Texas, can attract the attention of big players in the game. Many of the major publishers, philanthropic donors, educational policy makers, universities, and angel investors are represented at or are attending conferences like this one. SXSW hosts include the Bill and Melinda Gates Foundation, Microsoft, and McGraw-Hill Education, to name a few.

To develop your marketing video, webinar, or presentation, you need to be inspired. Even if you've already created your calling card, it would be wise to watch presentations from other inspiring people with unique ideas. It can shape how you present yourself if you study what works and what doesn't in others' presentations. Here are some places to view conceptual videos, and to develop the approach for pitching one of your own:

▶ *The Do Lectures* is an exciting venue is for "movers and shakers, disrupters and change makers" to tell their stories. It focuses simply on people who do amazing things. View www.thedolectures.com.

▶ *Capture Your Flag* is a video mentor series that helps those struggling through stages in their careers see that others have been there, too, and how they evolved. Do you have a career experience that would be helpful for others to know about? Maybe it belongs on Capture Your Flag (www.captureyourflag.com).

▶ *Talks at Google* showcases the most talented people of our time with autobiographical style speaker videos. See www.youtube.com/user/atgoogletalks.

▶ *The School of Life* is a forum where humans teach other humans what they know about the most important and interesting parts of living, which often involve mind-blowing concepts. There, speakers give presentations in London, but they have a video channel you can watch on www.youtube.com/user/schooloflifechannel.

▶ *The World Domination Summit* is a gathering in Portland, Oregon, that teaches mini-academies on interesting subjects, such as how to speak a new language in one day, simplifying your life, and how to spot great business ideas. In 2014 the conference drew 3,000 people and grows each year. View www.worlddomination-summit.com/story.

▶ *Chicago Ideas* is a premiere annual gathering of global thought leaders gathered to provoke new ideas and inspire results. Speakers are the leaders of our day in every category imaginable and take on deep, life-and-death topics that inspire. View https://www.chicagoideas.com/years/2014/videos.

▶ *Behance's 99U* wants to "empower the world to make creative ideas happen" by matching up talent to opportunity with their presentation series. View www.99u.com/videos.

▶ *The Royal Society for the Encouragement of Arts, Manufactures, and Commerce* (RSA) wants to enrich society through ideas and action. View www.thersa.org/discover.

▶ *TED-Ed*. Creating a video for TED-Ed gives you good practice in developing a piece you can use for multiple presentations. Here's the registration or nomination form: www.ed.ted.com/get_involved; and here's more about the program: www.ted.com/about/programs-initiatives/ted-ed.

Articles

Pitch an idea on an interesting topic to a magazine whose readers are your audience. Here are some ideas:

▶ AARP (www.aarp.org)
▶ *The Economist* (www.economist.com)
▶ FabJob.com (http://fabjob.com)
▶ *Writers Weekly* (www.writersweekly.com)
▶ *Women's eNews* (http://womensenews.org)

12

Tales from the Trenches

N one of the professionals who got into distance education could predict where their hearts would take them. Following their paths have led them to create projects that can be experienced all over the world and that can even change the world, by increments. Even though their contributions vary greatly, it seems the thing they have in common is a desire to share knowledge—that great kindness that is responsible for the evolution of our species today. Here are a few of their stories and sights on the future.

Change the World

Mitch Braff's filmmaking background producing works for PBS and corporate clients primed him for what would be a great contribution to eLearning. In 2000 he met a Jewish partisan and decided he wanted to capture this monumental part of Jewish history while Jewish partisans still lived to tell their stories. He then interviewed more than 50 Jewish partisans from around the world to create an educational series of videos illuminating the strength of the human spirit over bigotry and oppression, with the help of educators, filmmakers, and designers.

Braff also founded the Jewish Partisan Educational Foundation (JPEF, at www. jewishpartisans.org) in 2000, which educates students about these 20,000 to 30,000 Jews who fought back against the Nazis by "blowing up thousands of armored convoys and thwarting the Nazi war machine in countless ways. This information has the power to transform people's perception of the Jewish experience during the Holocaust." By spreading this information JPEF celebrates and encourages heroic resistance against tyranny. This program designed for grades 6 through 12 is being implemented in Jewish and secular schools worldwide. The series reaches more than 8,500 educators worldwide, supplying them with educational material on Jewish resistance. What a contribution to education!

In response to the completely preventable, high number of traffic deaths at railroad tracks, Operation Lifesaver, Inc. (OLI) of Alexandria, Virginia, created a series of interactive road safety training modules that act like video games. OLI targets training to professional drivers to help them make life-saving decisions at railroad crossings. According to spokeswoman Marmie Edwards, the education reaches somewhere around 100,000 of drivers per year and will eventually reach all truck drivers, saving countless lives. Some education actually saves lives.

In 1979 Dr. James "Milo" Milojkovic left his home in Melbourne, Australia, and travelled half-way around the world to pursue the remarkable adventure of earning a doctorate in psychology at Stanford University via full scholarship. "While I thoroughly enjoyed the rigors of a world-class graduate education, I still found it disquieting that I had to leave my family and friends in order to attend the lectures of my new professors. Little did I realize that this would spark a life-long interest in the profound challenges of education and the fascinating potential of a technology solution for distance education," says Milo.

After founding the first electronic university, The Electronic University Network, in 1985, Milo went on to eventually found his own leadership development and organizational transformation consultancy, KnowledgePassion, Inc., "With the advent of the internet [I] became once again fascinated with the potential of online learning, especially when broadband became available in people's homes. Through a partnership with the wonderful people at a German company, Mediacode GmbH, I co-designed a new, state-of-the art, private membership, video platform called Athena (www.athena.mediacode.net) designed primarily for me to use with my private executive clients at KnowledgePassion (www. knowledgepassion.com) and later made available for everyone who wished to showcase and sell their expertise online," Milo says. Athena serves as an education presentation platform with everything an educator needs to teach, and all materials easily accessible and organized for the student in a straightforward arrangement. The educator only has to deposit the content into the template and it is an almost instant, finished lesson. Teaching videos can be made on the spot and below the video are links to all related materials so conversations that refer to other sources are easy to have.

Live and Learn

It's possible to learn from the mistakes of others. Diane Elkins recounts some key aha! moments in her history as an eLearning professional. In the first case she learned how important keeping a close tab on finances is. "I know of two small businesses where an employee was embezzling money and another situation where a contractor was billing for hours not worked. So it's important to have checks and balances in place," Elkins says.

In terms of contracts and getting paid, Elkins has this to share: "I had a short-term project where we only did two billable milestones because it was supposed to be a six-week project. Because of client delays, it sat at 90 percent done for almost a year. We had incurred our costs for 90 percent of the work but had only been paid for 50 percent. So now we make sure we include more billable milestones, even on a short project. It doesn't mean we have to bill them separately—we might send one invoice for all milestones met that month, but we have the option.

"Another client had approved the course and we wrapped up the project. We sent the final invoice. Our contact left the company. Her boss got the invoice and wouldn't pay it until we could prove that we had our original contact that approved the work. Fortunately, we had her approval in the email. We learned to never make approvals verbally."

Julie Dirksen cautions about legal issues, "I think the legal issue that always comes up for me is the messy area of intellectual property—when I sign an agreement, what rights am I signing away? This is a particularly relevant issue for knowledge workers, as all their value is tied up in intellectual property. Handling intellectual property is a messy area in the legal system right now, anyway, given our current remix culture. I know other consultants who have walked away from work because the IP clause was too restrictive, and it's hard to know what is yours vs what is your client's when you do design work."

Carl Tyson believes that "interesting ideas attract interesting people. And again, it is really important to be working in the right type of place. In Austin there are many opportunities to share ideas with others and get feedback and to make connections. When someone makes a presentation at SXSW.edu they find dozens of people who are interested in the same areas and perhaps can become teammates. It is important, I believe, under any circumstances, for the founder or founders to have a clear vision they can express to others—that vision may change over time but it is difficult to attract talented people to your efforts without a clear mission statement.

"A lot depends on the situation in the local area—there are many different sorts of networks, but the important thing, again, I think is expressing a vision and attracting interest in how that vision might be built. The most important thing here . . . after having a great idea, is to spread it as widely as possible and talk to as many people in person or online about the vision. There will be many, many false starts but you have to persist. It takes a lot of work to get to the right mindshare with the right people. Does not happen quickly so you have to stay at it . . . even when it seems no one is listening.

"I have found key members via almost every route imaginable. Recruiters, web posting, chat rooms, trade shows. The key is to follow up with people. The first person you talk to might not be right but they can lead you to others and you can spread your network to find the right folks."

Salman Khan created a video lecture series for his nephew who was having a hard time with his studies and that led to Khan Academy, an incredibly successful website where students can access any kind of education immediately and chart a course to completing a module. The website keeps track of learners' progress and encourages them to finish. Khan said in a recent *Huffington Post* article that he will never tell his son that he's smart. He believes that struggling to learn makes the brain grow, much the same as working a muscle tears down the fiber and builds it back bigger than before. He is convinced that mindsets toward learning matter more than the subject matter and says researchers have "found that neural connections form and deepen most when we make mistakes doing difficult tasks rather than repeatedly having success with easy ones. What this means is that our intelligence is not fixed: and the best way that we can grow our intelligence is to embrace tasks where we might struggle and fail." What he wants people to know is that if they embrace struggles, they can learn anything. So go forth and create challenges for yourself and your students—growth is inevitable. We are looking forward to seeing what you create!

eLearning and Training Resources

Just as you can never have too many eLearning and training facilities from which to choose, you can also never have too many resources. Therefore, we present for your consideration a wealth of sources for you to check into, check out, and harness for your own personal information blitz as you prepare to make your mark in the eLearning industry. These resources will get you started on your research. They are by no means the only sources out there. We have done our research, but events, websites, and businesses tend to move, change, fold, and expand. As we have repeatedly stressed, do your homework. Get out and start investigating.

Associations

Association for Talent Development, (800) 628-2783, www.td.org, customercare@td.org

Center for Research on Education Outcomes (CREDO), Stanford University, (650) 725-3431, credoatstanford@gmail.com

Digital Citizenship Network, International Society for Technology in Education; http://connect.iste.org/connect/communities

International Council for Open and Distance Education, +47 22 06 26 30; http://icde.org, icde@icde.org

International Council on Archives, +47 22 67 33 99; www.ica.org/3/homepage/home.html

International Society for Technology in Education, (800) 336-5191; www.iste.org, iste@iste.org

National Federation of Independent Business, (800) 634-2669; www.nfib.com

United States Distance Learning Association, (800) 275-5162; www.usdla.org

Books

Clark, Dorie. *Reinventing You: Define Your Brand, Imagine Your Future*. Boston, MA: Harvard Business Review Press, 2013.

Dirksen, Julie. *Design for How People Learn*. San Francisco: New Riders, 2011.

Elkins, Diane, Desiree Pinder, and Tim Slave. *E-Learning Uncovered* series. Jacksonville, FL: Artisan E-Learning.

Halpern, Belle Linda and Kathy Lubar. *Leadership Presence: Dramatic Techniques to Reach Out, Motivate, and Inspire*. New York: Gotham Books, 2004.

Morrell, Ernest, Rudy Dueñas, Veronica Garcia, and Jorge López. *Critical Media Pedagogy: Teaching for Achievement in City Schools*. New York: Teachers College Press, 2013.

Wilson, Kenneth G. and Bennett Daviss. *Redesigning Education: A Nobel Prize Winner Reveals What Must Be Done to Reform American Education*. New York: Teachers College Press, 1996.

Consulting Services

The Ariel Group, 1050 Waltham Street, #600, Lexington, MA, 02421; (781) 761-9000. Helps business professionals develop presence.

Kristen Fyfe-Mills, senior manager, communications, Association for Talent Development (ATD, formerly ASTD), 1640 King Street, Alexandria, VA, 22314; (703) 683-8100; www.td.org

Tech Support

Burke Virtual Presence Support, Pariah Burke, (503) 422-7499; www.burkeassists.com. Provides support staff for presenters and facilitators, providing hosting, technical support, training, recording, post-production, documenting, etc.

Ed Tech Marketplace, www.edtechmarketplace.com. Database dedicated to education professionals, helping them find the products and services they need.

Net Support School, Classroom instruction, orchestration, monitoring and management, www.netsupportschool.com. Helps instructors manage classroom technology.

Test Prep Companies

BenchPrep: Learning management system using advanced analytics

Club Z! In-Home Tutoring Services: SAT/ACT prep

College Board: SAT/ACT prep/practice

C2 Education: Prep services for SAT, ACT, AP exams, et al.

empowergmat: GMAT prep course

Grockit: Test prep for GRE, GMAT, ACT, SAT, et al.

Knewton: Supporting differentiated instruction

Kaplan, Inc.: Online degrees and test prep

The Princeton Review: MCAT prep

Revolution Prep: Private tutoring, test prep

StudyPoint: SAT/ACT tutoring

Sylvan Leaning: Tutoring programs

Vestry Street Prep: LSAT tutoring

Events

Career Week, ASTD, www.td.org/Events/Career-Week. Annual event that highlights professional development resources—including podcasts, webcasts, and more—for training professionals.

Miami Device, www.miamidevice.org. Typically takes place in November each year, seminars on game-based learning, student-centered learning, and best practices in 21st-century education.

United States Distance Learning Association (USDLA) National Conference, www.usdla.org. Typically takes place in the spring of the year, providing opportunity to share ideas, learn about distance learning programs and products, and gain a better understanding of the field. Keynote speaker, sessions, posters, and panel discussions.

Free Training Guides, eBooks, Classes, and Lectures

EdX.org. Interactive online classes from universities/organizations

openculture.com/freeonlinecourses. Listing of free online courses, free ebooks, and other online learning possibilities.

philosophytalk.org/stations. Nonprofit radio program, deals with fundamental problems of philosophy and how the ideas of famous philosophers relate to today.

Virtual Presence, Making Authentic Connections with Virtual Audiences, www.arielgroup.com/virtually-connecting-authentically. A guide to helping virtual employees feel connected and engaged and making virtual meetings more productive.

Podcasts, MOOCs, and Webinars

Coursera.org. For-profit educational technology company offering open online courses

EdX.org. Interactive online classes from universities/organizations

iTunes U (www.ipadpd.com/itunes-u.html). Educational content through Apple's iTunes store

Iversity.org. Free online courses, European-based

Udacity.com. Online courses and "Nanodegree programs"

Udemy.com. Online courses

usdla.org/Webinars_s/1879.htm. Webinars from the United States Distance Learning Association

Job Opportunities and Talent Pools

Adjunct Professor Online, www.adjunctprofessoronline.com. One-stop resource to thousands of adjunct jobs posted by higher education job boards

Chronicle of Higher Education, http://chronicle.com/section/Home/5

Higher Ed Jobs, www.higheredjobs.com. "Online/remote" search category

Get Educated, www.geteducated.com. "Online education jobs" category

Indeed, www.indeed.com. Search "online teaching" or "online instructor"

Simply Hired, www.simplyhired.com. Search "online teaching"

Study Portals, www.studyportals.eu/careers. Publisher of education portals; based in the Netherlands

WAHM, www.wahm.com. Work-at-home moms online newsletter

Software and Learning Management Systems

Cengage, (800) 354-9706, www.cengage.com. Educational content, technology, and services company for higher education and K–12.

Designing Digitally, (866) 316-9126, www.designingdigitally.com. Custom eLearning, games, virtual worlds, and 3D training simulations for employee education and training.

Ed Tech Marketplace, www.edtechmarketplace.com. Resource directory from International Society for Technology in Education.

LaunchCycle, (800) 460-6494, www.launchcycle.com. Project management software.

Leo Kryon Systems, (646) 383-7887, www.kryonsystems.com. Real-time process automation support software.

Mindmarker, (855) 662-7537, www.mindmarker.com. Employee training reinforcement.

Newrow, (212) 354-5888, www.newrow.co.il. Interactive video platform.

Sumaria, (866) 786-2742, www.sumarianetworks.com. Global telecom and high-tech learning service organization.

Travitor, (888) 298-2070, www.travitor.com. Learning management software.

Welocalize, (800) 370-9515, www.welocalize.com. Translation and localization services.

Wisetail, (406) 545-4662, www.wisetail.com. Learning management system.

Xyleme, (303) 872-0233, www.xyleme.com. Learning content management system.

Successful Online Trainers

Mitch Braff, Jewish Partisan Educational Foundation, www.jewishpartisans.org

Julie Dirksen, Usable Learning, (612) 729-1927, www.usablelearning.com

Diane Elkins, Artisan E-Learning, (703) 679-8929, www.artisanelearning.com

Marmie Edwards, Operation Lifesaver, Inc., www.oli.org. Nonprofit safety education for driver awareness around railroad tracks and trains.

Salman Khan, Khan Academy, www.khanacademy.org

Connie Malamed, The eLearning Coach, www.theelearningcoach.com. Resources for designing, developing, and understanding online learning.

Dr. James Milojkovic, CEO KnowledgePassion, Inc., www.knowledgepassion.com, james.milo@gmail.com

Thinkwell Corporation, 3601 South Congress Avenue, Suite G200, Austin, TX 78704, (512) 416-8000, www.thinkwell.com. Online video learning specialists.

Trade Publications

American Journal of Distance Education, Taylor & Francis Online, www.tandfonline.com, six times/year.

Distance Learning magazine, www.infoagepub.com/distance-learning, quarterly.

ELearning magazine, www.2elearning.com.

Elearn magazine, www.elearnmag.acm.org. Online learning strategies, especially gaming.

Learning Solutions Magazine, www.learningsolutionsmag.com. Learning technology, strategy.

Training Magazine, www.trainingmag.com. Professional development.

Publishing Platforms,
Learning Management Systems

Academyofmine.com

Braincert.com

Click4course.com

Coggno.com

CourseMerchant.com

Digitalchalk.com

Dojolearning.com

Educadium.com

Edu20.org

Ezlcms.com

Inquisiqr4.com

Learningcart.com

Litmos.com

Kunerango.com

Mindbites.com

Mindflash.com

Myonlinecampus.org

Opensesame.com

Pathwright.com

Proprofs.com

Ruzuku.com

Scooltv.com

Skyprep.com

Udemy.com

Wiziq.com

Trainer Certification Programs

ATD Training Certificate, Association of Talent Development, www.td.org/Certification/
  ATD-Certification-Institute

Certificate Programs Training magazine, www.trainingliveandonline.com/2015/

The Innovator's DNA, www.innovatorsdna.com/offerings/

Td.org, www.td.org/Education/Programs/Training-Certificate

Glossary

Accreditation: Meeting essential education standards as required by a governing body

Apps: Electronic applications created as a minimized program for use on mobile devices

Asynchronously: Describes eLearning that is accessible whenever you like, in your own time frame

Chat room: An online forum where visitors can log in and talk in real time to each other

Common Core Standards Initiative: A set of unified expectations for K–12 education

Content: Material used in online publications and classes

Content provider: An author of online material

Cyberforensics: The use of recovered digital material in investigating criminal cases

Distance learning: Education obtained via electronic classrooms instead of at a physical site

eDiscovery: The process of seeking, locating, obtaining, and securing digital evidence to be used in criminal investigations

Educational technology: Electronics, both hardware and software, used in educational settings

Edupreneur: An entrepreneur in the education industry

Eduteam: A group of workers in the education industry tasked with a specific development or problem-solving activity

Encore roles: Second-, third-, or retirement careers

Fixed-time courses: Classes taught online but at a specific time where all students log in at once

Focus group: A group of typical users who help the marketing and development of a product by using prototypes and answering questions

Forum: An online discussion group often set up as part of an online class for students in the class to discuss a topic with each other

Gamification: Creating a learning experience by making use of electronic gaming technology

Generation X: Those born from the early 60s to the early 80s

Generation Y: Those born from the early 80s to the early 2000s, also known as Millennials

Hybrid courses: Combination of synchronous (real-time) and asynchronous (on your own time) e-classes

Instructional design: The creation of instructional experience that makes learning effective, efficient, and appealing

Laddering: In debt management, for example, laddering refers to paying your debts according to the highest interest ones first

Lifelong learning: Courses that are designed for appeal to all age groups and not just for the specific purpose of getting a degree toward a career path

Millennials: *See* "Generation Y"

Mind Maps: Visible tracking of the flow of a brainstorming session and the creation of new ideas

Platform: The electronic format by which the online class is structured

Portal: The point of access to the online course

Professional development: Classes for job training and on-the-job training

Self-paced learning: Courses that you do in your own time frame

Service Provider: This is the electronic host for your website that makes it function and do things you want it to do like sell products or courses

Syllabus: The outline of a class over the timeframe it will be taught

Synchronously: The accessing of eLearning in real time

Venture capital: Capital that provides start-up or growth opportunities

Webcast: A media presentation over the internet that distributes the presentation to many viewers

Webinar: An online class that can be viewed live by many participants or be watched later as a streaming video.

Index